CW01617562

GOOD HOUSEKEEPING
FAMILY LIBRARY

NEEDLEWORK FOR PLEASURE

Titles in the
Good Housekeeping Family Library
include:

Doing Up Your Home
Family Cookery
Family Health
Flower Arranging and House-Plants
Gardening
Home Medical Handbook
Jams and Preserves

GOOD HOUSEKEEPING
FAMILY LIBRARY

NEEDLEWORK FOR PLEASURE

Eileen Lowcock

SPHERE BOOKS LIMITED
30-32 Grays Inn Road, London, WC1X 8JL

First published in Great Britain in 1973 by
Ebury Press
First Sphere Books edition 1975

Cover picture by Camera Press.

ISBN 0 7221 3950 0

Grateful thanks are due to J and P Coats for their co-operation in the preparation of this book, for giving permission to reproduce several of their designs and for providing stitch diagrams for both the embroidery and crochet sections.

In the event of any queries concerning the yarns used in this book, write to the manufacturer concerned (for addresses, see page 115), who will be pleased to advise.

Filmsetting in Britain by
Typesetting Services Ltd, Glasgow.
Printed and bound in Belgium by
Henri Proost & Cie p.v.b.a., Turnhout.

CONTENTS

	Foreword	7
	Introduction	9
1	Embroidery	12
2	Canvas Work	42
3	Patchwork	59
4	Appliqué	71
5	Needle-made Rugs	86
6	Smocking	100
7	Making up and Finishing	112
8	Stitches	116
9	Crochet	122
10	Crochet Stitches	146
	Index	160

FOREWORD

Handwork of every kind is increasingly valued today, due to a revulsion against the mass-produced and the anonymous in clothes and furnishings. This is doubtless one of the reasons for the remarkable revival of interest in so many different branches of needlework.

But there is more to it than that to account for its present popularity. Something rather exciting has been happening to this formerly staid and static pastime in the last 20 years or so. In the first place, needlework design for the amateur has undergone a revolution: it has shaken itself free of the trite pre-occupations of the pre-war and immediate post-war years, the anaemic flower motifs, vapid crinoline ladies, crazy paving and sundials, windmills and clogs, thatched cottages and hollyhocks which used to appear in so many designs intended for the amateur needlewoman.

Although Needlewoman's Lib. is by no means complete—many commercial designs are still unimaginative, out of date and uninspiring—there is now plenty of scope for the amateur who is interested in good contemporary design or who wishes to experiment with her own ideas, as Eileen Lowcock shows in this book. In the second place, and even more significant, women who are now taking up needlework in their spare time are no longer doing so as a socially approved habit, but purely and simply for the fun of it.

Women of the leisured classes in the past seem sometimes to have turned to the decorative arts for a variety of reasons that had little to do with enjoyment. Penelope pining for Odysseus took to weaving; the wives of absent Crusaders stitched away at bed-hangings in draughty castles; Mary, Queen of Scots, and Catherine of Aragon turned to embroidery when in captivity; and Marie Antoinette drew threads from the sacking in her cell and made lace while waiting for news of the fate of her family.

Victorian daughters embroidered fire-screens and slippers while waiting for suitors, and when hope was finally abandoned turned their talents to embroidering hassocks and other church furnishings. Their little sisters, waiting to become adults, were set to work samplers: a practice which, in mid-Victorian England became a characteristically punitive method of keeping children quiet, teaching them the alphabet and improving their souls through the working of texts, all at one and the same time.

Few women find leisure hanging heavily on their hands in the 1970s, but many more than ever before can now spare time to devote to hobbies. So it is not surprising that we are turning again to needlework, but in a spirit of enjoyment rather than consolation. Today amateur needlework seems a much more cheerful affair, not so much a way of passing the time while waiting for something better as a pastime or recreation in the proper sense of the word. That is why we have called this book, NEEDLEWORK FOR PLEASURE.

Isabel Sutherland
General Editor
Good Housekeeping Family Library

INTRODUCTION

Anyone taking up needlework today has a very much wider range of materials to choose from than her mother had. New yarns are being produced all the time and synthetics obtainable now range from lurex to artificial raffia. But whether you choose to work in modern man-made yarns or in traditional silks, wools and cottons, the probability is that you will be using the same stitches that needlewomen have been working for generations. The uses to which you will put them and the designs which will appeal to you may be very different but basically the techniques will be the same. And if you are starting on a canvas work cushion cover, say, or a drawn fabric set of table linen, it can be both fascinating and instructive to go to a museum and look at a piece of work done in the same way. You will learn a lot about the principles of design that have been followed in the past. There is something very touching, in any case, about the work of a human being long dead and gone, quite irrespective of the beauty of the workmanship.

The great age of English embroidery

Englishwomen were already renowned for their needlework as far back as Saxon times. Among the spoils of the Norman Conquest were wonderfully embroidered robes worked in gold thread which were taken back to France by William the Conqueror. Embroidery, in common with other arts, was chiefly patronised by the Church at this period, so that religious themes predominate, in combination with flowers, fruit, birds and animals.

It was in the Middle Ages that English needlework reached the extreme height of perfection in the form of Opus Anglicanum (a Latin term meaning simply, English work). This gorgeous type of embroidery, which was in great demand throughout Europe, was used chiefly for church vestments. It was worked in silver or silver-gilt thread laid on a background of linen, silk or later, velvet and couched with linen or silk thread. Themes such as the Annunciation and the Virgin and Child were depicted together with animals, birds, foliage, cherubs and angels, all carried out in exquisite decorative naturalism.

Although there is a marked decline in the standard of church embroidery after the Black Death, embroidery continued to be used on the heraldic garments worn over armour. The trappings and clothes worn by the English at the Field of the Cloth of Gold became legendary. With the Renaissance, domestic embroidery flourished and reached new heights in the reign of Elizabeth I. And it was in the Elizabethan era, too, that the amateur needlewoman came into her own; embroidery had previously been mainly in the hands of professionals, some of whom were women but many of whom were men. Great households indeed continued to include a professional embroiderer among their retinue of servants.

Royal pastime

The Tudors had a taste for flower, fruit and foliage motifs worked on linen and then applied to silk or velvet. Canvas work in tent stitch or cross stitch was also popular and so was the more sombre black work or Spanish stitch, a technique in which motifs were embroidered on linen and other fabrics in black silk. Elizabeth I attired herself in stiff, jewel-encrusted embroidered garments, from dresses to gloves to slippers. The Queen herself worked a scarf for Henry IV of France and sent it to him with a disarming request that he 'look kindly' on its shortcomings.

The working of samplers by young girls became customary in the 17th century, but in the early days the serious and improving tone which became evident in the following century was absent. It was simply an exercise in and a record of a variety of different stitches. Allegorical and scriptural scenes were favoured by the Stuarts; there was also a vogue for portraits copied from oils. Decorative quilting was popular at this period; as was also crewel work. A strong Oriental influence, in particular Chinese, becomes clear in the needlework of the latter part of the 17th century. Such designs were often used on bed-hangings and curtains. White work, including drawn thread, showed no signs of waning.

Canvas work grew steadily in popularity through much of the following century, being greatly in demand for wall hangings and upholstery. The designs of the 18th century tended to be floral or pastoral, with a penchant for biblical or allegorical figures such as the Virtues. Women's dresses and indeed men's coats and waistcoats were decorated with delicately embroidered flower and bird designs worked in silks. The taste for sprigged muslin towards the end of the century led to the development of a special cottage industry specialising in embroidering these simpler designs.

Bright, but not beautiful

Needlework design by the middle of the 19th century was predominantly pictorial. Berlin wool work (a type of canvas work so called because printed designs for canvas work were first issued by a Berlin firm) became tremendously popular. Much use was made of tent stitch, cross stitch and a clipped stitch which formed a pile. The colours used were often bright and rather crude and the designs tended towards the tastelessly florid. They included elaborate flower pieces assiduously shaded to give a 'lifelike' effect, scenes from the Bible, historical events and portraits of the royal family. Even patchwork and appliqué were often pictorial at this period, designs being based sometimes on contemporary prints.

Among those who deplored the vulgarity of mid-Victorian needlework were William Morris and the painter Edward Burne Jones. They were determined to revitalise embroidery design and turned to the Middle Ages for inspiration. Morris set up his own firm, had wools specially dyed and produced wall hangings and panels in formal patterns based on flowers and leaves. The founding of the Royal School of Needlework in 1872 led to a new awareness of the importance of good design and proved the death knell of the florid extravagances of the Berlin wool work. Art needlework, as the new movement came to be called, was characterised by delicate flower and bird designs which were as restrained as their predecessors had been crudely over-stated.

These movements which did so much to improve design had nevertheless in some respects looked back over the shoulder. It was not until the end of the last century that a truly original school developed under the direction of the breakaway designer Charles Rennie Macintosh. Rejecting tradition, they evolved a highly stylised type of design akin to art nouveau. Yet much fine needlework continued to draw on the designs of the 17th and 18th centuries for the next 20 years or so.

Lively and exciting

Modern painting began to have a considerable effect on professional needlework design of the Twenties and Thirties, but regrettably did not affect to any great extent the designs which were available to the amateur. These were often boring, insipid and cliché-ridden, despite the efforts of a number of organisations to educate and improve taste in this field. The advent of Pop Art in the early Sixties, together with influences from the continent, were two factors which helped to produce the present livelier and more exciting trend in design.

Today the accent is on richly and boldly decorated abstract designs worked in a variety of yarns, colours and stitches; the opportunities and scope for the needlewoman nowadays are virtually limitless. This is an exciting and stimulating development but at the same time a slightly heady one; with an ever widening choice of materials and range of designs, one needs to exercise discretion and self-discipline to avoid confusion.

The 19th century needlewoman's conviction that there is an intrinsic value in painstaking, tedious work irrespective of its merits has practically disappeared (and a good thing too). A number of the very effective designs that follow do not in fact take long to work and are suitable for anyone whose spare time is precious.

There are, as you will have gathered from this short outline of English needlework, a great many different branches, each one having its own set of techniques. This book sets out to present a cross-section of the currently most popular.

1 EMBROIDERY

If you try to do any kind of embroidery without the right equipment, you will be making things more difficult for yourself. With the wrong type or size of needle, for instance, the work itself will be hard going and you will probably be disappointed with the result. So here is a guide to some of the tools and materials you will need, together with an explanation of the basic techniques used in embroidery.

Before you start

Needles

To ensure the best results, always use the correct needles for the type of work in hand. For general sewing with sewing cotton, use a Sharps needle, medium length with a small eye.

Crewel: A long, sharp needle with a long, narrow eye. Use sizes 6–8 with stranded cotton, coton à broder, pearl cotton No 8 and stranded pure silk. Use size 5 for crewel wool and pearl cotton No 5.

Chenille: A short, sharp needle with a large, long eye for thick yarns such as soft embroidery cotton, crewel wool, tapisserie wool or knitting yarns.

Tapestry: A needle with a blunt point used for canvas work, counted thread embroidery and for whipped and laced stitches.

Beading: A very fine, small-eyed needle used for sewing on beads.

Thimbles, scissors and tweezers

Do get used to wearing a thimble as this assists in the correct control of the needle. When working with an embroidery frame, one thimble should be used on each hand. Make sure that it fits comfortably and is not damaged or rough. Thimbles are made in different sizes and are obtainable in plastic, nickel or silver. For embroidery, a plastic thimble may feel a little bulky; nickel or silver are better.

It is really well worth investing in the best scissors you can afford. A good-quality pair of scissors will last almost a lifetime, whereas a cheap pair will soon be worn out and will not do the job properly in any case.

A pair of stainless steel dressmaker's scissors will be needed for cutting out fabrics. A pair with 3-inch blades are useful for cutting yarns. A small pair of embroidery scissors with fine, pointed blades will be needed for fine work and in embroidery where threads or sections of the fabric have to be cut out, as in drawn thread work or cut work. A pair of eyebrow tweezers is useful for pulling out small pieces of yarn when unpicking is necessary.

Embroidery frames

Most embroidery is best worked using a frame, as the fabric is held taut and the stitches rest evenly on the surface of the fabric. There are two main types of embroidery frames, a tambour frame which is round and consists of two rings, one of which fits firmly inside the other and a slate frame which is rectangular. The slate frame is preferable because it allows both hands to work the stitiches and because larger areas of fabric can be framed at one time, giving the worker a better view of the work as it progresses.

Tambour frame: There are three kinds of tambour frame; the embroidery screw ring kind which is held in the hand, the kind which clamps on to a table and the table frame kind which has a stand. To prepare the tambour frame for use, take the inner, smaller ring and wind bias binding evenly all round it, completely covering the wood. This ensures a firmer grip on the fabric when it is set in the frame and protects the fabric from marking. Place the inner ring on a table and the fabric to be embroidered over it and press the outer ring down over the inner ring. Gently but firmly ease the fabric taut in the frame, keeping the grain of the fabric straight in both directions. Tighten the screw and the fabric is ready to be worked. If a delicate fabric is being used, cover it with a sheet of white tissue paper before fitting the outer ring. When the outer ring is in position and the fabric taut, tear back the tissue to the edge of the frame.

Slate frame: A slate frame consists of four strips of wood, two strong, rounded cross-bars joined with two flat side-bars with peg holes at intervals to vary the size. There is another type of rectangular frame which has threaded side-bars for screwing the fabric taut. These are suitable for only the lightest of fabrics because the screw rings tend to work loose as the embroidery is in progress and have to be tightened frequently.

There are two kinds of slate frames on the market, hand frames which are set on trestles for working, and floor-standing frames. The hand frame can easily be supported by the back of a chair on one side and a table on the other, instead of using trestles. Hand frames are available in sizes ranging from 18–28 in. and floor frames from 24–30 in. Certain suppliers will accept orders for making frames to any required size. (*See Useful Addresses*, page 115.)

To mount fabric in a slate frame first mark the centre of the webbing on the rollers with tacking stitches. On the top and bottom of the fabric to be mounted, make a $\frac{1}{2}$ in. turning to the wrong side. If the fabric is likely to fray, make a hem. Mark the centre of the fabric each way with a line of tacking stitches. Place the centre of the top and bottom edges of the fabric to the centre of the webbing and pin from the centre outwards.

Using very strong cotton, threaded double in the needle, oversew the two edges together, working from the centre outwards in both directions. Insert and adjust the side-bars until the fabric is taut. Tack 1 in. wide tape to the side edges of the fabric, using a double thread and small stitches. Thread a large chenille needle with strong string and lace through the tape and over the slats with stitches 1 in. apart. Leave about 18 in. of string free at each end. Pull the string up taut and wind it round the ends of the frame. Tie to secure.

Improvised frames: A canvas stretcher used by painters or an old, plain picture frame can be improvised as an embroidery frame. The fabric is simply laced vertically and horizontally with string to the frame.

Fabrics

It is possible to use almost any fabric for embroidery but those with a dull surface are generally better than shiny ones such as satin or brocade. If a charted design is being worked for counted thread embroidery or drawn thread work, an evenly woven fabric is essential, i.e., one with an even number of vertical and horizontal threads to the inch. There are 'even weave' fabrics made especially for embroidery but many linens, cottons and rayons in both dress and furnishing fabrics are also of an even weave and these are equally suitable. Do check before starting the design because if the fabric is not of a precise, even weave the design will be distorted.

Yarns

There is a wide variety of yarns available for embroidery today and the choice need not be limited to those yarns made specifically for embroidery. Knitting, crochet and weaving yarns are all useful and are available in a variety of textures, ranging from smooth double knitting yarn to slub and tweed textures and lurex yarns. String, plastic, raffia and even threads unpicked from woven fabrics can all be put to use. There are always new yarns coming on to the market and it is just a matter of experimentation to see how best to use each one. Here is a general list of yarns for the various types of embroidery and suggestions for using them.

Anchor linen: A fine, twisted, shiny linen suitable for cut work, pulled thread work, drawn thread work and smocking.

Soft embroidery cotton: A thickish, twisted, matt cotton suitable for couching, Hardanger work, simple stitches, pattern darning and canvas work.

Coton à broder: A fine, twisted, shiny cotton suitable for pulled and drawn thread work, cut work, Hardanger work, smocking, white work and basic embroidery stitches.

Crewel wool: A fine worsted yarn, twisted, matt, with two or more strands threaded in the needle. Used for crewel embroidery, couching, canvas work and needle-made rugs.

Slub cotton: A knitting cotton with an uneven thick and thin texture.

Can be used for couching.

Tapisserie wool: A twisted, matt wool suitable for couching, basic stitches, pattern darning and canvas work.

Stranded cotton: Fine, twisted, separable and shiny. Used for most basic stitches, counted thread work, pulled and drawn thread work, Hardanger and canvas work.

Pearl cotton: A twisted, shiny cotton available in two thicknesses, No 8, thin and No 5, thick. Can be used for counted thread work, drawn and pulled thread work, Hardanger, smocking and canvas work.

Mohair: A fluffy knitting yarn which can be used to a limited extent for basic embroidery stitches. It is also suitable for couching.

Metallic threads: These are available in a wide variety of different types, some of pure gold, some with a percentage of gold and others made of silver or lurex. Suitable mostly for couching, though some of the finer varieties can be used for simple stitches. Lurex knitting yarns can be used for embroidery or canvas work.

Raffia: Plastic raffia is suitable for couching, some simple stitches and canvas work.

Pure silk: A lustrous stranded yarn suitable for fine embroidery, counted thread work and canvas work.

Ryagarn: A firmly twisted woollen yarn used for canvas work and rug-making. It can also be used for bold, simple stitchery.

Rug wool: A thick, 6-ply wool for rug-making.

Thrums: A 2-ply woollen yarn used for canvas work and rug-making. It can also be used for couching in embroidery. Thrums are the ends of wool left over from carpet-making and are described as either 'Brussels' or 'Axminster'. They are of good quality and fairly inexpensive.

Preparing your fabrics

All fabrics need a certain amount of preparation before any embroidery can be begun and this is time well spent. Most benefit from pressing to remove centre fold marks or small creases. Press them on the wrong side over a dry cloth to remove slight creases and over a damp (not wet) cloth for stubborn creases. Velvet should always be pressed over a velvet board, again, on the wrong side, or steamed in front of a kettle. If the fabric is likely to fray at all, the edges should be oversewn or temporarily hemmed before being embroidered.

It is essential to mark the centre of the fabric before placing any design. This is done by working a line of tacking stitches across the centre of the fabric both horizontally and vertically. The centre guide lines are then matched to the centre lines of the design when it is being transferred to the fabric.

Mounting: Many fabrics benefit from being mounted on a fabric such as unbleached calico or holland to give added strength and to prevent the weight of the embroidery puckering the background fabric. This is particularly necessary for appliqué, metal thread embroidery, wall hangings and pictures. The calico or holland must be pre-shrunk by pressing well under a damp cloth before it is used. The background fabric is then tacked to the backing. Work vertical and horizontal lines of tacking at the centre of the fabric and all round the edge. The two layers are then treated as one fabric.

Testing for colour fastness: Do check fabrics for colour fastness, especially for appliqué and patchwork. Take a snip of fabric, dip it in water, lay it on a piece of white fabric and iron it dry. If any colour 'bleeds' on to the white fabric, the colour will run when the fabric is washed. Fabrics which are not colour-fast should be dry cleaned and not washed.

Transferring designs

Commercial transfers are available in a variety of designs but many of these tend to be both out of date and out of step with modern trends in embroidery. It is much more satisfying to be able to select and work an original design of your own, so it is worth learning how to transfer designs on to fabrics by means of the following simple techniques. You will find it easier to transfer a design when the fabric is held taut in an embroidery frame.

Tacking method: This is suitable for designs with simple outlines. Trace the design on to a sheet of tracing or greaseproof paper and mark the centre both vertically and horizontally. Pin the design on to the fabric carefully matching the centre lines of the design to those of the fabric. Using Sylko or pure silk, matched to the background fabric, tack the outlines of the design through the paper on to the fabric. When all outlines have been marked in this way, carefully tear away the paper. If the embroidery stitches completely cover the tacking lines, these need not be removed when the embroidery is completed.

Using carbon paper: Ordinary carbon paper should not be used as this will smudge and mark the fabric. A special type made for dressmakers is obtainable and this is the type to use. Black, blue and red are used for light and medium coloured fabrics and yellow for darker fabrics. Trace the design on to tracing or greaseproof paper. Mark the centre of the design and fabric both vertically and horizontally. Lay a sheet of carbon paper on to the fabric and then place the traced design on top, matching the centre lines of both design and fabric. Pin or tack smoothly in place. Using a hard, sharp-pointed pencil, trace over all the outlines carefully. Remove the design and carbon paper.

Direct tracing: This method is useful for sheer and semi-sheer fabrics, such as organza. Trace the design on to tracing or greaseproof paper. Mark the centre of the design and fabric both vertically and horizontally. Pin and tack the design underneath the fabric and trace its lines directly on to the fabric, using a finely-pointed, hard pencil.

Enlarging and reducing

It is extremely useful to know how to alter the size of a design, whether you create your own or adapt them from those found in embroidery books or magazines. Even if you cannot draw, you will find it quite easy to get

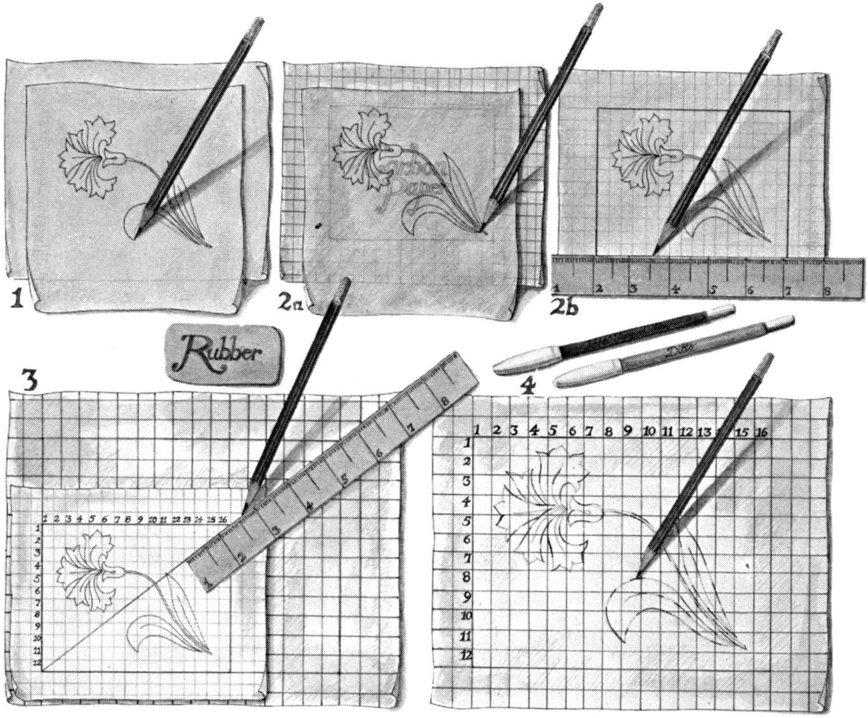

satisfactory results with this method. You will need some tracing paper, graph or squared paper, rubber, ruler, a Biro or felt-tipped pen and a soft leaded pencil.

Trace the outline of the design on to tracing paper, and then draw a rectangle round the design. Draw a diagonal line through the rectangle. Extend the two adjacent sides of the rectangle to the size you want the design to measure. Then draw lines at right angles from the ends of the extended sides to meet at an angle into the same number of squares as are in the small one to form a grid. Draw the grid in pen as it may be necessary to rub out and re-draw some of the lines of the design to improve the shape.

In pencil, carefully copy the design on to the larger grid. Make tiny marks on each square of the grid where the lines of the design cross it, then join up these marks (see diagrams above).

To reduce a design, use the same method in reverse.

Learning to handle colour

Some people are naturally gifted, or have been trained to use colours, but many others are uncertain, especially in the early days, about how to choose a colour scheme for a particular piece of work. However, the more embroidery you do, the easier colour selection will become. It is best to start off with one colour on a self-colour or contrast background and to use different tones of that colour or a selection of textured yarns. As you gain experience, try gradually bringing in one or two more colours. Avoid using too many colours in one design as the eye will be confused with a mass of colour and distracted from the design itself; this is one of the most common mistakes when beginning embroidery.

If you are not sure about a colour scheme, it is a good idea to work a section of the design on to a piece of the background fabric to see if the colours are suited to the design. If you are stuck for ideas, you will find that printed or multi-coloured woven fabrics, paintings or fashion shades are a useful source of inspiration for planning colour schemes.

Starting and finishing off

Many people have difficulty in carrying out the simple operation of threading a needle, often because they are not using the right size and type of needle for the particular yarn. Pull a length of yarn from the skein or ball and thread this end into the needle; if you thread the other end you will find that the yarn tends to twist whilst working. For tightly twisted yarns such as coton à broder or SYLKO, you will need to wet the end of the yarn in the mouth and give it a little nibble to flatten it slightly. (Don't, incidentally, ever be tempted to bite off thread instead of cutting it or you may damage your tooth enamel.) Dampen the thumb and first finger of the left hand, straighten the yarn and then with the right hand thread it through the eye.

For woollen or stranded yarns, hold the needle in the left hand as before, then take the end of the yarn and fold it over the needle. Pinch the folded yarn between the thumb and first finger of the right hand and insert it into the eye. Don't try to work with too long a thread or it will be difficult to handle and the constant pulling through the fabric will wear it thin, resulting in uneven work. A length of 12–18 in. is advisable, depending on the type of yarn being used.

When starting to work, first make a knot in the end of the yarn. Insert the needle from the right side of the work about 2–3 in. along the line of the design. Bring the needle up to begin the embroidery. When the yarn has been worked over, cut off the knot and trim the yarn close to the back of the work. There should be no knots left in the finished piece. Alternatively, leave a length of yarn on the right side to start with, and take it to the back of the work and darn it in after the line of stitching has been completed. Finishing off is done by a similar method; as the end of the yarn is reached take it to the back of the work and darn it in to the back of the stitches for about ¾ in. before cutting off.

A Selection of Embroidery Designs

Here are working instructions for making all sorts of attractive furnishings for your home, from place mats to curtains to bedcovers. The selection is planned to include a wide variety of embroidery techniques; instructions and diagrams for the stitches used are given in Chapter 8.

Cross stitch napkins (See below, pages 20–21, and 153–5)

This set of cross stitch motifs for table napkins was designed to harmonise with cushions, curtains and table mats made in contemporary printed fabrics. A single motif is embroidered in one corner of each napkin; the motifs could equally well be used to decorate other small items. For each napkin measuring 14 in. square, you will need:

A 15-in. square of linen with 20 threads to 1 in.
Clark's Anchor Stranded Cotton: 1 skein each in the colours listed against the colour symbols of each working chart.
A crewel needle No 8.

To make

Stitch a narrow hem on all four edges of the fabric. Mitre the corners (see Chapter 7). Following the chart, begin the embroidery 30 threads (1½ in.) above one corner of the napkin. Start at the lower part of the motif, using three strands of cotton in the needle; work each cross stitch over two threads of fabric each way. (For stitch instructions see Chapter 8.)

Key to charts

Chart 1	dark blue 0149	●
	sky blue 0141	○
	dark green 0244	▲
	light green 0208	∧
	brown 0370	×
Chart 2	yellow 0298	●
	red 047	●
	light red 0335	▲
	pink 029	×
	light pink 076	○
	lilac 093	▼
Chart 3	yellow 0298	○
	light orange 0315	●
	dark orange 0326	×
	green 0281	■
Chart 4	yellow 0305	●
	mustard 0308	○
	brown 0339	▼
	green 0281	×

1

2

(For enlargements of charts 1, 2 and 3, see pages 153–155

3

Atlantic Press

4

Wavy-bordered curtains (See below and page 24)

Curtains display embroidery to good advantage. This bold design with its flowing lines is carried out in simple stitchery. You will need:

A pair of curtains in brown linen.
Clark's Anchor Pearl Cotton No 8, 1 ball each of green 0255 and red 046.
Crewel needle No 7.

To work

Using the carbon paper method, transfer the design (see diagram 5) on to the right side of the fabric, 5 in. in from the inside edge of the curtain. Work the design throughout in either chain stitch or stem stitch (see Chapter 8).

5

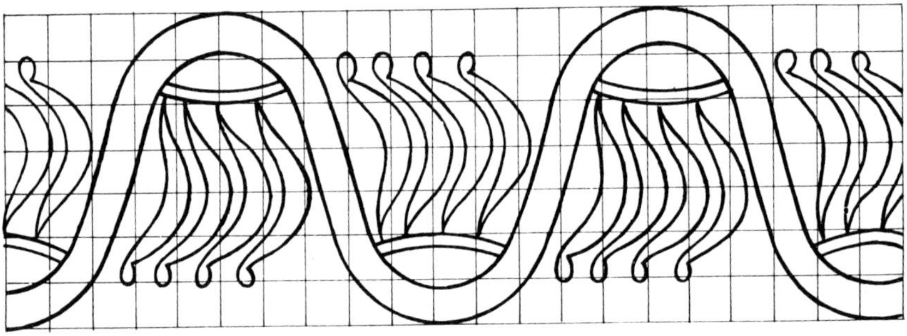

Water lily table cloth (See opposite and page 24)

This charming circular table cloth is embroidered with a single water lily framed with leaves. The design is worked with three simple embroidery stitches but it would translate equally well into appliqué (see Chapter 4). The table cloth measures 44 in. in diameter. To make it you will need:

$1\frac{1}{3}$ yds even weave linen 45 in. wide in ice blue.
9 yds bias binding to match linen.
Crewel needle No 7.

Clark's Anchor Stranded Cotton in the following colours and quantities: 1 skein each A cream 0300; B pale cream 0386; C pink 048; D light blue 0158; E white 0402; two skeins each of F mustard 0279; G light grey-green 0858; H grey-green 0215; J green 0210; K dark green 0211.

To work

Make the cloth following the instructions given in Chapter 7. Enlarge the design from the chart (6) and transfer it centrally on to the cloth, using either the carbon paper or tacking methods (see *Before you start* in this chapter). The flower is worked entirely in long and short stitch, the stems and leaves in chain stitch. All the leaves are outlined with a single row of stem stitch worked in the predominant colour of each leaf.

6

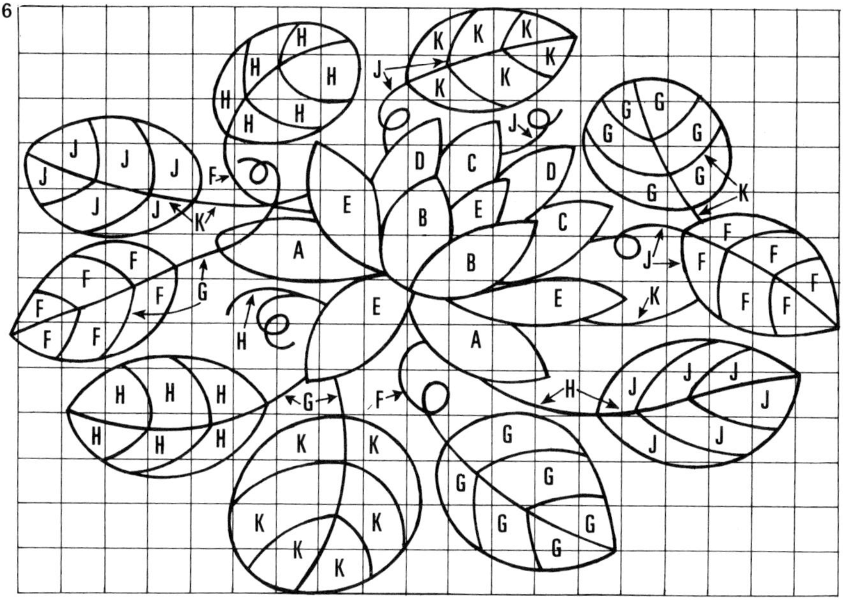

Fruits and berries table runner (See page 24)

A variety of fruits and berries worked in a subtle shading of colours makes a delightful design repeated down the centre of this table runner. The same design could be used for a picture to mount and frame. To make the runner you will need:

A strip of even-weave linen 14 in. wide in the required length in white.
A crewel needle No 7.
Clark's Anchor Stranded Cotton, 1 skein in each of the following colours for one repeat of the design: dark olive 0281; yellow-green 0279; pale yellow 0295; pale pink 048; yellow-green 0265; green 0257; yellow 0289; bright pink 052; red 058; orange 0304; lilac 0107; lilac 0122; dark turquoise 0170; turquoise 0169; red 047; blood red 046; pale green 0259; white 0402; pale blue 0120; dark olive 0281; pale green 0241.

To work

Enlarge the design (7) to measure $9\frac{3}{4}$ in. by 6 in. (see *Before you start* in this chapter) and transfer it centrally on to the runner, repeating as many times as required. The entire design is worked using three strands of cotton in the needle. The subtle shading is achieved by using a mixture of strands in different colours in the needle at one time. Stitch all areas in long and short stitch unless otherwise stated (for stitches, see Chapter 8).

1 Pear: Stitch with yarns ranging from dark olive to pale pink, shadow

Atlantic Press

Above: *Wavy-bordered curtains* (see page 22)

Below: *Water lily table cloth* (see pages 22 and 23)

Camera Press

7

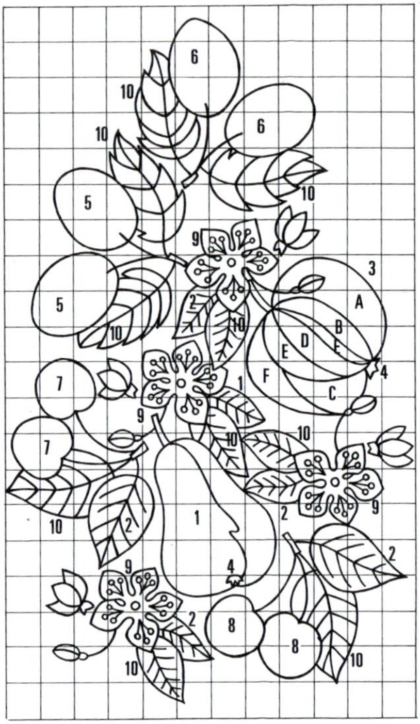

Above and below: *Fruit and berries table runner* (see previous and opposite pages)

Camera Press

with 2+1 strands and use colours: 0281; 0279; 0295; 048. Outline in stem stitch using 0281.

2 Leaf: 0265, veins in stem stitch 0257.

3 Apple: (a) 2 strands 0289+1 strand 0279. (b) 2 strands 048+1 strand 0289. (c) 1 strand 048+2 strands 052. (d) 1 strand 058+2 strands 052. (e) 3 strands 0279. (f) 3 strands 0304, outline in stem stitch with 3 strands 052.

4 Apple: and pear cores: 3 strands 0107.

5 Plums: one green, one lilac. First plum: 3 strands 0122, outline in stem stitch 0170. Second plum: 3 strands 0279, outline in stem stitch 0169.

6 Plums: two in dark turquoise. 3 strands 0170, outline in stem stitch 0169.

7 Cherry: 3 strands 047, outline in stem stitch 046. Work stalk in stem stitch 0259.

8 Cherry: 3 strands 047, outline in stem stitch 046. Stalk, stem stitch 0259.

9 Flower: 2 strands 042+1 strand 048. At bottom, outline in stem stitch with 1 strand 0120. Work stamen with 2 strands 052, pistil and anthers with 2 strands 0281.

10 Leaf: 3 strands 0241, veins in stem stitch 0259.

Make up the runner in the same way as for a table cloth, mitring the corners (see Chapter 7).

Lupin and marigold picture (See below and page 26)

Four stitches are used to work this engaging bunch of flowers and foliage;

Coats

its rich colours are offset by being mounted on a dark background. The wall picture measures 15¼ in. by 20¼ in. You will need:

A piece of fine black felt measuring 19¼ in. by 24¼ in.

Clark's Anchor Stranded Cotton: 1 skein each carnation 024; petunia 092 and 094; parma violet 0109; periwinkle 0117 and 0118; kingfisher 0159; laurel green 0210 and 0212; canary yellow 0288; amber gold 0306; orange 0324 and cinnamon 0371.

A crewel needle No 6.

A piece of cardboard measuring 15¼ in. by 20¼ in.

A piece of mounting board measuring 15¼ in. by 20¼ in. (window in mount to measure 7¾ in. by 12 in.).

A frame measuring 17 in. by 22 in., width of frame 1¼ in., and two rings.

To make

Embroider the design (8) following the diagram key. When the embroidery is completed, press the work on the wrong side. To mount and frame the picture, see instructions in Chapter 7, *Making up and finishing*.

Key to diagram

1 = 0210	} Stem stitch	
2 = 0212		
3 = 0159	} Satin stitch	
4 = 0117		
5 = 0118		
6 = 024		
7 = 0109		
8 = 092		
9 = 094		
10 = 0210		
11 = 0212		
12 = 0371		
13 = 0288	} Long and short stitch	
14 = 0306		
15 = 0212		
16 = 0324	— French knots	

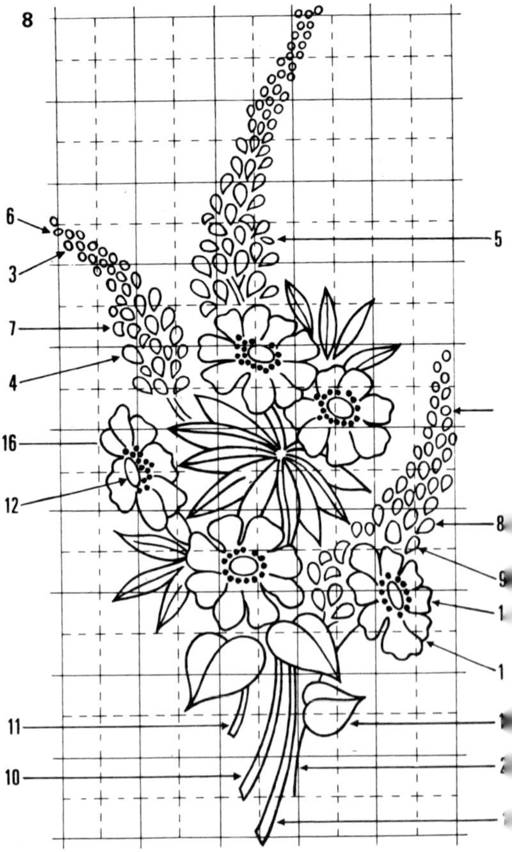

Drawn fabric table sets (See below and pages 28–9)

This crisp, white table cloth and napkins set is embroidered in drawn fabric work which comes under the heading of counted thread embroidery. Even weave fabric, which has an exact number of threads each way to a sq. in. is used, the stitches being worked over the counted thread. The finished effect appears quite intricate but the stitches used are easy to work. They are shown off to best effect if you keep to a monochrome scheme. So, if preferred, the design could be worked on blue with blue stitchery or any other colour, provided the stitchery is worked in a tone of the same colour as the fabric. The table cloth measures 56 in. by 69 in. or 51 in. by 69 in. and the set of napkins measures 13 in. square. You will need:

2½ yds white even weave linen with 21 threads to the in., 59 in. or 54 in. wide. (The size can be adjusted to fit individual requirements.)

Clark's Anchor Pearl Cotton No 8 (10 gram ball): 3 balls white 0402, for embroidery.

Clark's Anchor Pearl Cotton No 5 (10 gram ball): 2 balls white 0402, for satin stitch only.

1 each *Milward 'Gold Seal'* tapestry needles Nos 23 and 21 for Pearl Cotton Nos 8 and 5 respectively.

To work

Cut a 75 in. piece from the fabric for the table cloth and three pieces measuring 15 in. square from the remaining fabric for the napkins. Mark the centre both ways on each piece of fabric with a line of tacking stitches; these lines act as a guide when placing the design. The working chart (10) gives the centre of the design, the centre being indicated by blank arrows which should coincide with the tacking stitches on the tablecloth. The working chart also shows the arrangement of the stitches on the threads of the fabric

9

which are represented by the background lines.

The layout diagram (9) shows left half of the design for the table cloth, the centre being indicated by broken lines which should coincide with the tacking stitches. The lettering on the layout diagram indicates the sequences of the three fillings worked within the motif marked X on the working chart. The section on the left of the layout diagram inside the dotted outline is worked on the napkins. Follow the working chart and number key for the design and stitches used and the layout diagram for the placing of the design. (Fillings A, B and C must be pulled firmly.)

The stitches used are A—double faggot stitch filling, worked over two

Drawn fabric table set (see previous page and opposite)

Coats

1
2
X

threads of the fabric, B—linked four-sided stitch filling, C—coil filling stitch. The other two stitches used are 1, satin stitch and 2, whipped back stitch (for stitch instructions, see Chapter 8).

With the long side of the fabric facing, begin the design centrally and work the section given on the working chart. Turn the fabric and work the other half in the same way. To complete, work the fillings in the positions indicated on the layout diagram. When commencing fillings B and C, the cloth must be turned, so that the narrow end of the fabric is facing. Each filling is worked from the extreme right hand side of the shape. Begin the design for the napkin at the black arrow on the layout diagram, 101 threads down and 13 threads to the right of the crossed tacking stitches, and work the section within the dotted outline, following the working chart for the design and stitches used. To complete, work the other three corners in the same way. Press the embroidery on the wrong side.

To make up: Trim the margins even. Turn back 1 in. hem on the table cloth and ½ in. hems on the napkins, mitre the corners and tack. Work hem stitch over 4 threads round each article to secure the hem in position.

Apple embroidered cushion (See right and page 32)

This bold, effective design is carried out in simple stitches and is quite quick to do. Shown here on a cushion cover, it could equally well be used for curtains or other furnishings. The cushion measures 20 in. square. To make it you will need:

A piece of red linen measuring 21¼ in. square.
A piece of white linen measuring 21¼ in. square.
Clark's Anchor Pearl Cotton No 5: 1 ball each of yellow 0298; green 0242; white 0402.
Sewing cotton—red.
A crewel needle No 7.
A zip fastener measuring 16 in.
A cushion pad measuring 22 in. square.

To make

Transfer the design (11) on to the centre of the red linen. Using Pearl Cotton, double throughout the embroidery, work the design in chain stitch, making each stitch about ¼ in. long. Begin in white at the stalk and the outer edge of the apple. Next work rows of chain stitch in yellow to fill the left hand side of the apple, starting at the outer edge and working towards the centre. Fill in the small centre at the right in the same way. Work the flowers in white or yellow and the stems in green. The outer edge of the flowers are worked in chain stitch and the centres filled in with straight stitches (for stitches, see Chapter 8). Press on the wrong side. To make up, follow the cushion cover instructions given in Chapter 7.

1

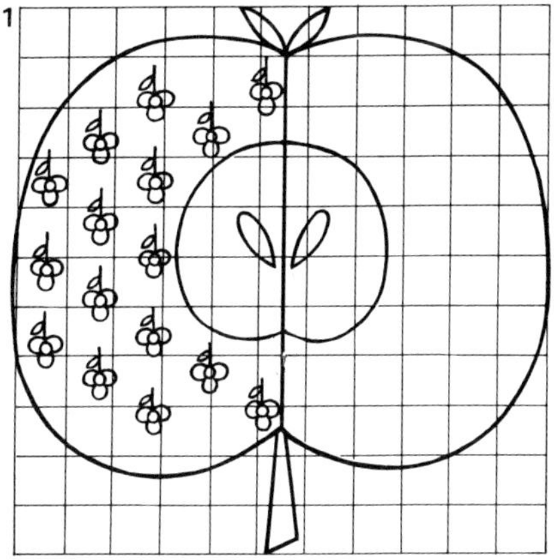

12

Spring flower table mats (See above and pages 32–33)

Fine, white linen is used for these pretty, flower-embroidered table mats in two shapes, a simple rectangle and a scalloped oval. To make the mats you will need:

For the rectangular mat: A piece of fine, even weave linen measuring 18 in. by 12 in.

For the oval mat: A piece of fine, even weave linen measuring 20 in. by 14 in.

Bias binding to match linen.

For both mats: *Clark's Anchor Stranded Cotton*, 1 skein of each of the following colours to work one mat: dark green 0281; light green 0278; gold 0306; dark mauve 0873; light mauve 091 and light pink 095.

Sewing cotton to match linen.

A crewel needle No 8.

To work

Make a plain, narrow hem on each edge of the rectangular mat and mitre the corners. Trace, enlarge and transfer large flower design (14) on to the left hand side of the mat (see *Before you start* in this chapter for enlarging and transferring). For the oval mat, trace outline (12) and enlarge. Transfer the outline on to the fabric and cut out, leaving $\frac{1}{4}$ in. turning on all edges. Finish the raw edges with bias binding stitched round, pressed down and hemmed to the wrong side of the mat. Make sure that the binding does not show on the right side of the mat. Trace, enlarge and transfer motif (13) right side up on the left hand side of the mat and upside down on the right hand side as shown.

Using three strands of cotton in the needle, work the stems in chain stitch, the left hand row in gold, the right hand row in dark green. The out-

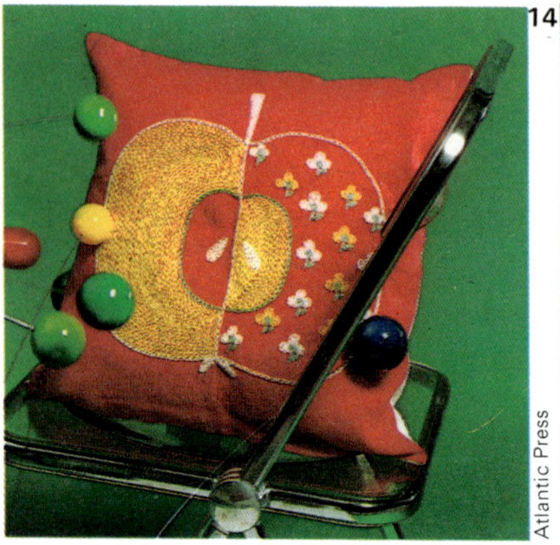

Above: *Apple-embroidered cushion* (see pages 30–31)

14

13

Above and left: outlines for *Spring flower table mats* (see page 31); below: detail.

line of the leaves and flowers are also in chain stitch, using two strands of the cotton for a fine line. The veins of the leaves are worked in stem stitch, the inside of the petals and leaves are in long and short stitch and the centre of the flower worked in satin stitch. Alternate dark and light green leaves, and light and dark pink flowers. When all the embroidery is completed, press the work on the wrong side.

Below: *Spring flower table mats* (see page 31 and opposite)

Atlantic Press

Pink-flowered bedspread (See below, right and over)

This bedspread, embroidered in shades of pink and yellow, is quickly worked in simple stitches, using crewel wools. If you would rather use your own colour scheme, use tones of the colours you prefer. You will need:

A plain, single size bedspread in a coarse, even weave fabric.

Appleton's Crewel Wool, 1 skein of each of the following colours for working one motif: green 311, 313, 316; white 991; pink 943, 944, 946; yellow 554, 552; red 501, 502; and tan 766.

A crewel needle No 22.

To work

There are three different flower motifs (15, 16, 17); see details of two overleaf. The motif with the single large flower is repeated down the centre of the bedspread and each alternate motif is reversed. The other two motifs are

15

16

Above, left and opposite: Diagrams of the three motifs used in the *Pink-flowered bedspread* shown on page 36

7

worked down either side and also reversed alternately.

Using two strands of crewel wool in the needle, the leaves are embroidered in long and short stitch (for stitches, see Chapter 8) and the three shades of green intermingled. The veins and the stems of the branches are in stem stitch, using only one strand of wool in the needle.

Above: two of the motifs used in the *Pink-flowered bedspread* (see pages 34–35) shown below.

The small flowers are worked in long stitches in pink and red, with the base in green. The centre of the large flower in pink and yellow is embroidered with French knots in yellow, white and pink. The small petals in yellow are also worked in long stitches. Then, small French knots in red are worked between the yellow petals and at the base of the pink petals, which are embroidered in long and short stitch, light pink on the outside and dark pink at the base.

The centre of the other flower motif is worked with French knots in white and in the two shades of red. The petals are worked in white and pink with some stitches in red worked down the centre of each one. The stems are in stem stitch and worked with dark green wool.

When all the embroidery is completed, press on the wrong side under a damp cloth.

Peony bedspread (See below and overleaf)

The flower design on this bedspread achieves its effect by the subtle use of beige, ranging from the palest creamy beige to deep, golden tones. Here the design is shown worked and repeated down the centre of the bedspread but

Atlantic Press

it could be arranged in any order desired. It is worked in long and short stitch. You will need:

A plain, single size bedspread in coarse even weave fabric.

Anchor Tapisserie Wool. For each motif: 2 skeins each pale beige 0376; beige 0377; dark beige 0378; light tan 0398; tan 0351; and 1 skein maroon 0341.

A chenille needle No 18.

To work

Trace and transfer the design (18) repeated down centre of the bedspread. The flowers and leaves are worked in long and short stitch (for stitches, see Chapter 8) shading the different tones of beige for the petals and the tans and maroon for the leaves. The centre of each flower is worked in satin stitch surrounded by French knots. The stems and veins of the leaves are in stem stitch, a single row for the veins and several worked closely together for the stems. When all the embroidery is completed press the work on the wrong side.

18

Blackwork luncheon set (See opposite and pages 40–1)

A form of counted thread embroidery, blackwork—as its name suggests—is usually carried out in black on a plain background. Here, for a striking contrast, it is worked on red linen. To make this luncheon set consisting of 1 runner measuring 11 in. by 31 in. and two place mats measuring 11 in. by 16 in. you will need:

$\frac{1}{2}$ yd red, medium weight even weave fabric, with 21 threads to 1 in., 59 in. wide.

9

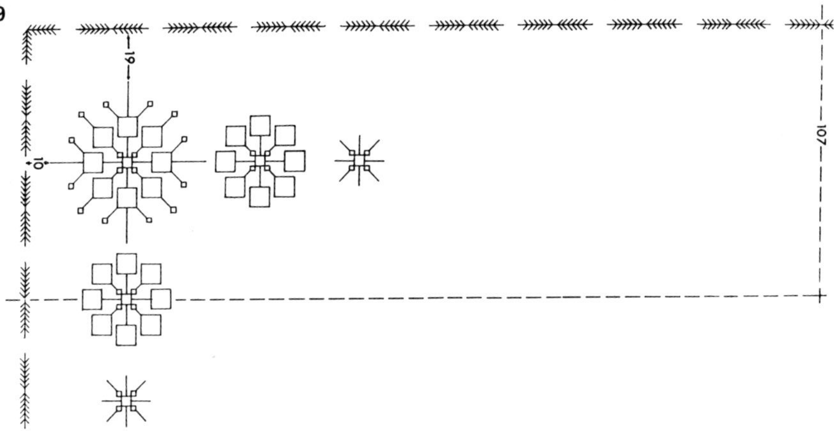

Clark's Stranded Cotton: 3 skeins black 0403 (use 3 strands in the needle throughout).

A tapestry needle No 23.

To make the set

Cut two pieces from the fabric measuring 13 in. by 18 in. for the small mats and one piece measuring 13 in. by 33 in. for the runner. Mark the centre both ways on each piece of fabric with a line of tacking stitches.

The working chart (20) gives the three motifs and rather more than half the border design and corner turning for the small mats; the centre lengthwise tacking stitches are indicated by a blank arrow. The working chart also shows the arrangement of the stitches on the threads of the fabric represented by the background lines. The layout diagram (19) shows the placing of the border and the motifs on a little more than a quarter of the runner; the centre is indicated by broken lines which should coincide with the tacking stitches. The numerals give the number of threads between the motif and the border. Follow working chart and number key for the design and stitches used.

Key to working chart

1 back stitch; **2** four-sided stitch; **3** straight stitch; **4** wheat-ear stitch and **5** fern stitch.

To work

With long side of the small piece of fabric facing, begin the design on the lengthwise tacking stitches 101 threads to the left of the crossed tacking stitches and work the section given on the working chart. Repeat the given section in the same way on to the right-hand side of the fabric, reversing the corner turning. Complete the border by repeating the section within

20
2
1
4
3
5

the bracket 8 times on each long side and 5 times on each narrow end, plus the corner turnings.

With the narrow end of the long piece of fabric facing, commence centrally on the widthwise tacking stitches 107 threads to the left of the crossed tacking stitches and work the border design and the motifs following the layout diagram. Turn the fabric and work on the other narrow end in the same way. Complete the border pattern. The section within the bracket on the working chart is repeated 17 times on each long side and 5 times on each narrow end, plus corner turnings.

Trim the margins even and press the embroidery on the wrong side. Work $\frac{1}{2}$ in. hems on all edges, leaving 4 threads of fabric between the border and the finished edge.

Below: *Blackwork luncheon set* (see page 38); left: working chart

2 CANVAS WORK

Embroidery worked on a foundation of canvas or linen fabric is known as canvas work; it has been produced in England since the Tudor period. Early examples show fine, intricate designs worked in a skilful blending of a variety of stitches. Canvas work remained popular until the middle of the 18th century when it fell out of favour because of the monotonous use of tent stitch to make slavish copies of flower pictures, landscapes and portraits imitating tapestry.

Recently, canvas work has enjoyed a revival. Once again the lovely variety of traditional stitches are being worked into striking modern designs, often carried out in a variety of yarns not formerly associated with embroidery. It makes a tough, hard-wearing fabric which can be used for all sorts of things from chair covers to fashion garments. Canvas work should not be confused with tapestry, although it is often mistakenly called such. Tapestry is always woven in sections on a loom to form patterns and pictures; the small sections are woven separately and then stitched together to form the completed panel.

Equipment

Scissors: Two pairs of sharp scissors are required, one for cutting out the canvas and a small pointed pair for cutting the strands of yarn.

Needles: Those with a long eye and a rounded point, sold as tapestry or rug needles, are available in a variety of numbered sizes. The smaller the number, the coarser the needle. Nos 18 and 20 are the most useful to have and No 14 is ideal for grafting canvas or for use with thicker yarns. No 26 should be used for finer yarns such as stranded silk or cotton. Packets of needles in mixed sizes can be purchased but these contain mainly fine needles used for very fine mesh canvas. The eye of the needle should be large enough to take the yarn freely and the needle itself of a size large enough to draw the yarn smoothly through the canvas without strain.

Thimble: To protect the finger from constant pressure and friction with the needle and to ensure that the needle is being held in a correct manner, a well-fitting thimble is essential.

Tweezers: A pair of eyebrow tweezers will be found useful for taking out cut wool when unpicking is necessary.

Graph paper: The type with 8 or 10 squares to 1 in. is ideal for drawing designs as each square on the paper can be taken to represent one stitch completed over two threads of the canvas.

Tape measure: A steel tape measure is preferable as this is useful for checking the measurements of the completed work.

Tracing paper: This is useful for copying designs from freehand sketches. The traced design can be transferred on to graph paper, outlined and squared off.

Slate frame: A good, strong slate frame is essential for all but the smallest pieces of work.

Canvas

There are two main types of canvas; single thread and double thread (sometimes called Penelope canvas). Canvas is made from cotton, Italian hemp or linen, the latter being the strongest. The canvas should be firm, supple and of a precise, even weave (having an equal number of threads to 1 in. in both warp and weft). The number of threads per in. can vary from 26 threads to 1 in. for very fine work, to 3 holes to 1 in. for coarse work such as rugs. It is also possible to use evenly woven fabrics such as Hardanger fabric, Aida cloth and even-weave linens.

Single weave canvas is measured by the number of threads to 1 in. and double thread canvas by the number of holes to 1 in. It is generally preferable to use single weave canvas since it is possible to embroider a great number of different stitches on it, whereas double weave canvas is restricted to the use of a mere four or five.

Yarns

In canvas work the stitches should completely cover the canvas for practical items such as bags but in modern designs for wall panels areas of canvas are frequently left bare as an integral part of the design. Yarns are available in varying thicknesses and some are composed of several strands; to cover the canvas it is important to select the correct thickness of yarn or number of strands.

The basic yarns used in canvas work are crewel wool which is stranded (never use less than 2 strands in the needle), tapisserie wool and pure stranded silk for extremely fine work. Stranded cotton, pearl cotton, soft embroidery cotton, PERLITA, gold and silver threads, lurex, plastic raffia and even string are all suitable for use in canvas work. For a comprehensive list of yarns suitable for canvas work see Chapter 1, *Embroidery*.

In modern designs texture forms an important part of the work and this can be achieved by the use of different stitches in one piece of work, or by the use of a variety of textured yarns, or by a combination of both. Don't feel you must use the yarns specified for any particular type of work. New yarns are constantly appearing on the market, so keep an eye open for unusual ones and experiment with these on a spare piece of canvas, trying out different stitches to discover which look the most attractive worked in that particular yarn.

Calculating quantities: It is possible to work out fairly accurately how much yarn will be needed to complete a charted design. Cut a skein of yarn into 18 in. lengths and if it is a stranded yarn divide it into groups of two, three or four strands (depending on how many strands you intend to use). Thread the group of strands into a needle and work the stitch until the end of the yarn is reached. Count the number of stitches worked and multiply this by the number of lengths of yarn in one skein. This gives the total number of stitches which can be worked with one skein of yarn in a particular stitch. (Different stitches will use up more or less yarn.) By counting the number of stitches to be worked in that colour from the chart, it is possible to calculate the quantity of yarn required to complete the design. It is always better to err on the side of too much rather than too little, as dye lots can vary considerably and the difference will show clearly in the finished work.

Preparation

When planning any piece of canvas work, measure the overall size required and add at least 1½ in. on all edges for stretching and seam allowance. The canvas should be worked with a raw edge top and bottom and a selvedge running down the left and right hand sides. Oversew the raw edges to prevent fraying. If the canvas is to be worked in the hand, cover the raw edges with tape or paper folded over and tacked in place. This prevents the yarn catching on the rough edges of the canvas.

Mark the top of the work. Then using a coloured thread in the needle tack through the centre both horizontally and vertically, following the grain of the canvas and working over and under 4 threads. Tack the outline of the actual shape required, counting the threads of the canvas out from the centre lines. Mount the work in a slate frame (instructions are given in *Before you start* in Chapter 1). Then trace the design on to the canvas or follow the design from a working chart.

Working in a frame: It is advisable to work all but the smallest pieces of canvas work in a slate frame. The use of a frame helps to keep the canvas true to shape; it holds the canvas stretched taut so that the stitches lie in an even tension on top of the work. As the stitches are worked in a stabbing movement, the use of a frame has the additional advantage that it allows both hands to be used for making the stitches. The right hand remains on top of the frame, inserting the needle, and the left hand remains beneath the frame, to receive and return the needle to the right side of the work for the next stitch. A tambour frame is not really suitable for canvas work as it distorts the shape of the canvas and it is almost impossible to stretch the canvas really taut for working.

Tracing a design on to canvas: Trace the design on to a sheet of strong white paper and outline it with black paint, Indian ink or a fine felt-tipped pen. Mark the centre lines on the design. Then pin the design on to a drawing board and place the canvas over it. The centre lines of the canvas should be matched exactly with those on the design and secured in this position with drawing pins. The rest of the canvas should be gently eased from the centre outwards and pinned down securely all round with drawing pins. The work is now ready for tracing. Tilt the board up against a table with the light coming from behind the person who is going to trace the design. The design should show through the canvas clearly; if any difficulty is found in seeing the design, shade the canvas with the left hand against light coming from above.

Using a fine sable paint brush and black watercolour paint, trace the design on to the canvas. Use the paint on the dry side and keep the traced line as fine and dark as possible. (If the design is simple, a fine felt-tipped pen can be used to trace the lines.) The brush or pen should be used with a slight scrubbing motion and held in an upright position.

Starting and finishing a length of yarn

Using an 18 in. length of yarn in the needle, make a knot at one end. Insert the needle from the right side of the canvas a couple of inches to the right along the line of design. Bring the needle up and begin the design, working over the yarn held under the canvas. When the yarn has been covered with stitches, cut off the knot and trim the yarn closely to the back of the work. Continue working the design until the end of the yarn is reached. Take the needle to the back and turn the work to the wrong side. Slide the needle under several stitches on the wrong side, first in one direction for about ½ in. and then back again. Pull the yarn firmly but not too tightly and trim off the end of the yarn close to the work.

Some yarns tend to twist whilst working; if this is not corrected at each stitch the finished result will be rough and uneven in texture. Check the yarn constantly and give it a few twists now and then when necessary. Other yarns wear thin or become fluffy from being drawn to and fro through the rough canvas. If this occurs, do not use the length of yarn to the end, as this will also result in uneven work with either thin, bare patches or fluffy, matted ones. Using a slightly shorter length of yarn in the needle should help.

Always start at the centre of the design and work outwards. This is important because the worked stitches 'spread' the threads of the canvas. If a section is worked from the outside inwards, the unworked threads of the canvas become tightly overcrowded in the middle and are impossible to work. In canvas work the central motif or design is worked first and the background filled in afterwards.

Stitches

There is a wide variety of canvas work stitches to choose from and a selection of these is included in the following designs. Most of the stitches are worked over 2 (or a multiple of 2) threads of canvas. Some are worked from left to right, some from right to left and others diagonally. The important thing to remember is that the work must never be turned sideways whilst working. It

1

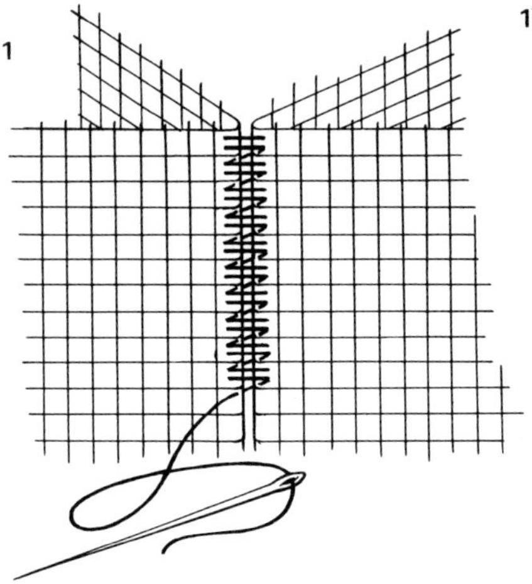

1a

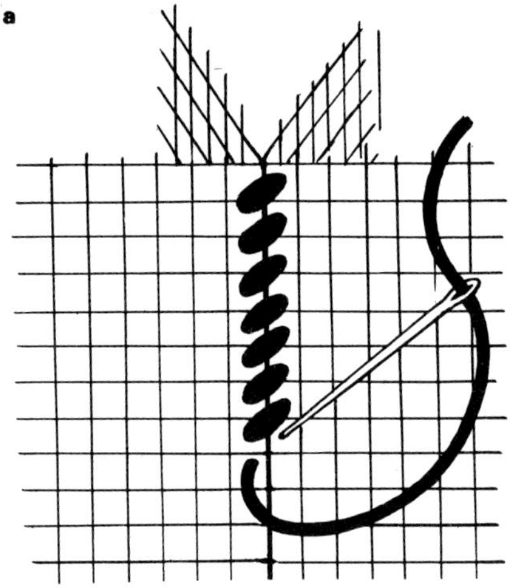

is therefore always advisable to mark the top of the work using a coloured thread. Check the work continually to ensure that all the top stitches slope in the same direction, usually from bottom left to top right. Any mistakes should be unpicked and re-worked; if they are left, they will appear very pronounced in the completed piece of work. When the work is finished (but before stretching) hold it up to the light to check whether there are any stitches left unworked.

Any new stitch that you want to try out should always be practised before working it on the actual design. It is a good idea to work two samplers, one to practise the stitches on and the other to keep as an example of each stitch worked in different types of yarn. Instructions for some canvas work stitches are given in Chapter 8.

Joining canvas

Most types of canvas are made in widths varying from 12 in. up to 36 in. wide and a few measure up to 44 in. wide. So if a large piece of work is planned the canvas will have to be joined. This is quite simple to do and the join should be invisible if carried out as follows. Fold back along a thread of canvas $\frac{1}{2}$ in. on each of the two edges to be joined together. Thread a needle with strong linen thread or button cotton to match the canvas and join the two pieces together as shown in diagrams 1, 1a. After the join is made work over it in tent stitch or whichever stitch is used in the design. Continue working through both thicknesses of canvas at either side of the join.

Stretching

Canvas work should never be pressed with an iron as this flattens the texture of the stitches and can completely ruin a piece of work. The diagonal pull of many of the stitches used in this type of embroidery usually distorts the shape of the canvas; most pieces of canvas work benefit by being stretched.

Cover a flat surface such as a drawing board or an old unpolished table with a clean towel, or several sheets of white blotting paper. Place the work right side down on this padding and thoroughly dampen it by dabbing with a sponge and clean water; but be careful not to soak the work. This initial dampening makes the canvas more flexible and easier to handle during the succeeding stage.

Using the straight edge of the board as a guide, commence at the centre on one long side and pin securely with rustless drawing pins, gently but firmly pulling and pinning from the centre outwards, left and right alternately, at intervals 1 in. apart. Continue in the same way along the next side until the whole piece of work is pinned firmly into shape. If the work has dried out slightly during this process dampen it again evenly all over. Cover the work with another clean towel or several sheets of blotting paper and weight it evenly with books or some other heavy flat object such as a suitcase. Leave to dry for at least 48 hours.

When the work is completely dry, remove the pins and trim the excess canvas to the required seam allowance (not less than $\frac{5}{8}$ in. on fine canvas and not less than 1 in. on coarse canvas). Oversew all raw edges to prevent fraying before making up. If the work is to be mounted as a picture strengthen the edges by binding them with folded tape stitched firmly in place.

Canvas work bed cover (See overleaf)

This unusual bed cover is worked in vivid-coloured wools in a patchwork-like design. To make a single size bed cover you will need:

8 yds double mesh canvas with 6 holes to 1 in., 23 in. wide, joined into a rectangle measuring 96 in. by 60 in.

Anchor Tapisserie Wool: 1–1$\frac{1}{2}$ lb in each of the following colours: mustard 0308; bright green 0265; tobacco 0348; orange 0334; terra cotta 0412; yellow 0297; and $\frac{1}{2}$ lb in blue-green 0507.

A tapestry needle No 18.

To work

Each motif is embroidered separately. Start the first one 6 holes in and 6 holes down from the edge at the left hand upper corner. To form the motif see diagram 2 and work as follows:

Thread the needle with a 40 in. length of wool. Bring the needle up at No 1 on the diagram, insert the needle at 2. Bring the needle up at 3 and insert the needle at 4. Bring the needle up at 5 and insert the needle at 6. Continue in this manner working the 44 marked squares on the diagram following the normal sequence of numbers (1, 2, 3, etc.). End in the 44th hole with the wool at the back of the canvas. Secure the end firmly. When the motif is worked, there are 4 holes free in the centre of each side. To fill them, work 3 straight stitches perpendicular to each side. These stitches are worked throughout in blue-green wool.

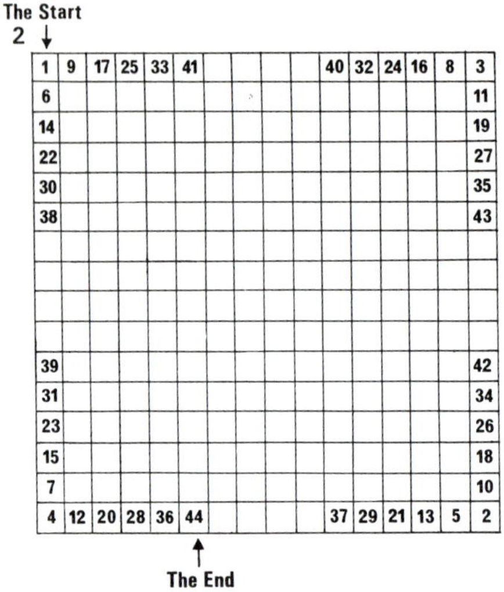

Below: *Canvas work bed cover* (see previous page); above left, method of working motif; right: detail

Placing the colours

ROW 1 One motif each *terra cotta, mustard, bright green, tobacco*, repeat *–* to within 6 holes of the edge of the canvas.

ROW 2 One motif each *orange, yellow, orange, mustard*, repeat *–* to end of row.

ROW 3 One motif each *yellow, terra cotta, yellow, bright green*, repeat *–* to end of row.

ROW 4 One motif each *tobacco, bright green, mustard, yellow*, repeat *–* to end of row.

Alternate these four rows until the canvas is covered, leaving 6 holes free all round for turnings. When the bed cover is completely embroidered fold the unworked canvas to the back of work, leaving 3 holes on the right side. Mitre the corners (see Chapter 7, *Making up and finishing*). Make a border by working rows of back stitch through the double layer of canvas.

Florentine cushion (See below, overleaf and page 156)

Rich, warm colours are used for this traditional flame design Florentine bolster cushion; its clean lines go well with modern furnishings. The cushion measures 21 in. long and 21½ in. in circumference. You will need:

¾ yd single thread canvas, 23 in. wide with 18 threads to 1 in.

Anchor Tapisserie Wool in the following colours and quantities: 8 skeins

Florentine cushion (see above); for working chart and layout see overleaf

Coats

tan 0351; 7 skeins each orange 0332; light red 0334; 6 skeins each yellow 0313; dark brown 0359; 5 skeins lime 0290; 4 skeins pale yellow 0288; 3 skeins white 0402.

$\frac{1}{4}$ yd yellow velvet 36 in. wide for ends of cushion.

$1\frac{1}{4}$ yds dark brown cord about $\frac{1}{4}$ in. thick for edging.

Cushion pad to fit cushion.

2 circles stiff cardboard 7 in. in diameter.

A tapestry needle No 18.

To work

Mark the centre of the canvas both ways with a line of tacking stitches. The chart (3) gives one motif, the centre being indicated by blank arrows which should coincide with the tacking stitches. The background lines on the chart represent the threads of the canvas. The layout diagram (4) gives half of the design, the centre marked by broken lines which should coincide with the tacking stitches. The Florentine stitch is worked throughout over 4 threads of the canvas. Follow the working chart and sign key for the embroidery. Begin the design centrally and work the section given. Complete one half following the layout diagram. Work the other half to correspond.

3

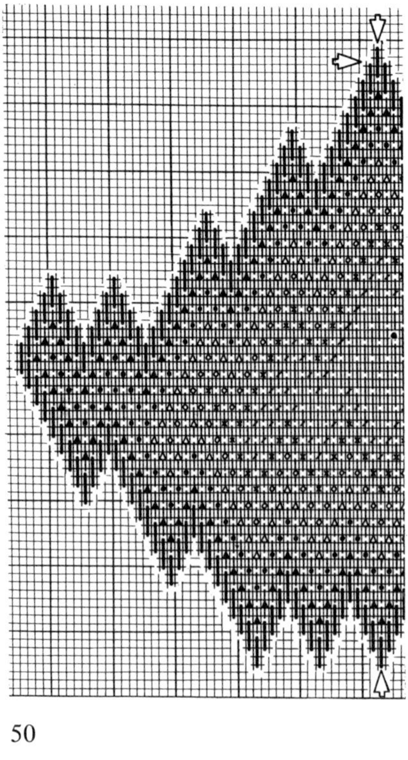

4

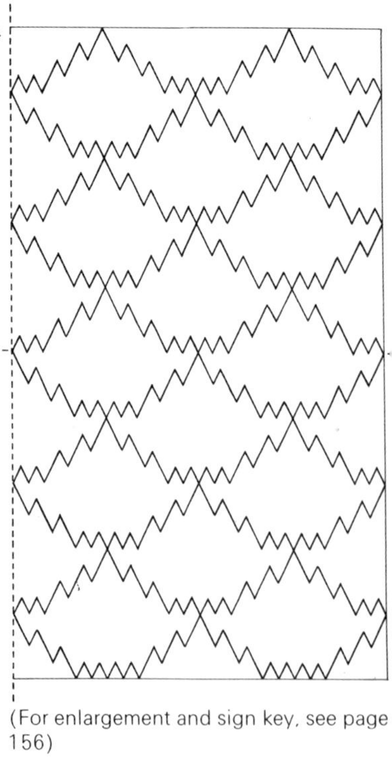

(For enlargement and sign key, see page 156)

To make up

Trim the canvas to within 1 in. of the embroidery at raw edges. Fold the selvedges in half, wrong side out, and machine stitch raw edges close to the embroidery. Turn to right side. Insert cushion pad. Cut two circles of velvet 9 in. in diameter. Work a row of gathering stitches $\frac{1}{2}$ in. from the edge. Place the cardboard pieces centrally on the fabric and pull up the gathering thread until the fabric lies taut on the cardboard. Secure at the back by lacing from side to side. Turn in raw edges on embroidered section and oversew the ends in position. Sew cord round the seam at both ends.

Abstract cushions (See below and pages 52–53)

These dramatic cushions decorated in bold, abstract designs are worked on coarse canvas in large-scale tent stitch and are quick and easy to make. The designs can also be used in a wide variety of arrangements to create individual designs for rugs. The cushions measure 18 in. square. For each cushion you will need:

A piece of double mesh canvas measuring 23 in. square with 6 holes to 1 in.
A piece of tweed fabric measuring $19\frac{1}{4}$ in. square in a dark shade.
Anchor Tapisserie Wool in the colours shown on colour key.
A zip fastener measuring 14 in.
Cushion pad measuring 20 in. square.
A tapestry needle No 18.

To work

Trace and enlarge the design and transfer the outline to canvas (see Chapter 1 for enlarging and transferring). Using 3 strands of wool in the needle, work the chosen design in tent stitch (see Chapter 8). When all the work is com-

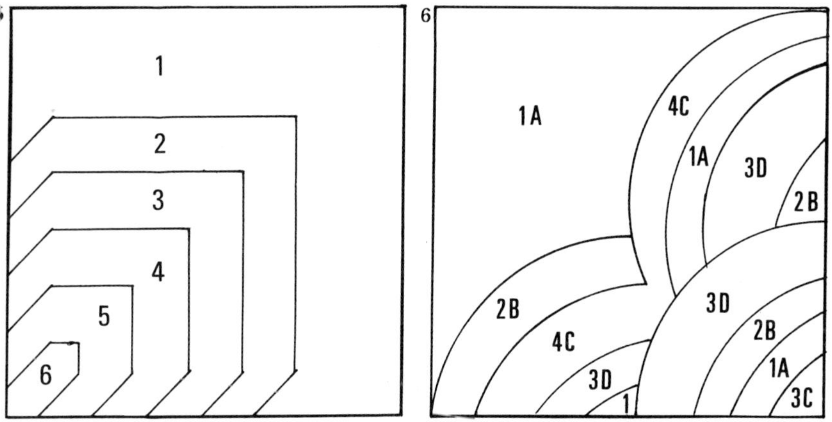

Above: *Abstract cushions* (see previous and opposite pages)

7

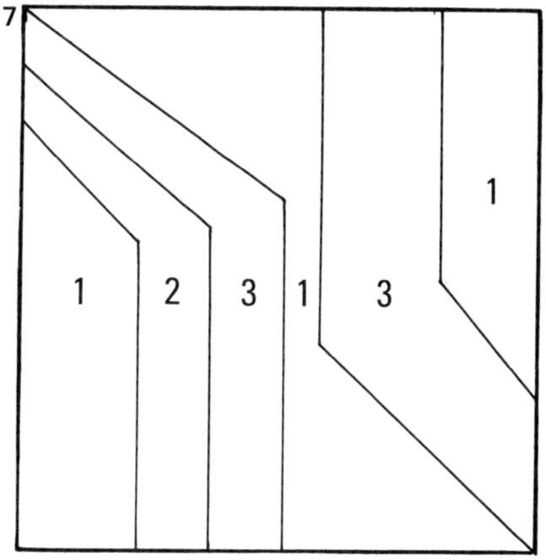

8

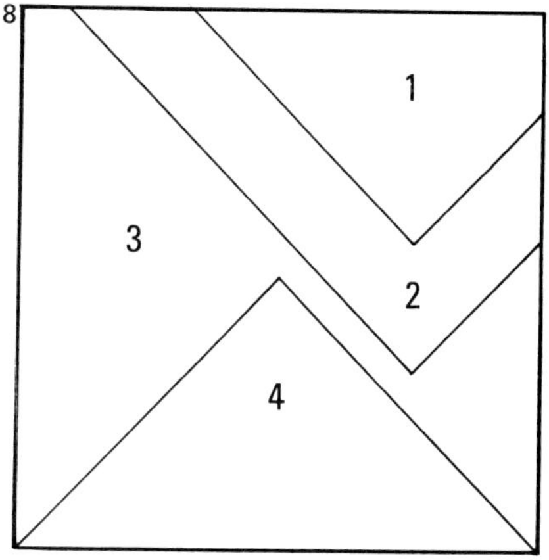

pleted stretch the canvas. Trim the excess to within 1 in. of the embroidery. Instructions for making up the cushions are given in Chapter 7.

Colour key

Triangles (diag. 8)
1 = bright red—0412
2 = dark navy—0851
3 = white—0386
4 = bright red—0412

Zigzag (diag. 7)
1 = white—0386
2 = burgundy—0430
3 = wine—0897

Arcs: red tones (diag. 6)
1 = white—0386
2 = burgundy—0430
3 = wine—0897
4 = burgundy—0430

Arcs: brown tones
A = white—0386
B = light tan—0501
C = bright red—0412
D = black—0403

Arrow (diag. 5)
1 = dark tan—0341
2 = white—0386
3 = wine—0897
4 = burgundy—0430
5 = violet—089
6 = lilac—0105

Rocking chair cushions (See overleaf and page 56)

These matching cushions for the back and seat of a rocking chair are tailored to fit neatly. The eye-catching geometric design, here worked in vivid colours, could equally well be used for other cushion shapes. To make the cushions you will need:

Double mesh canvas with 6 holes to 1 in., in the length and width required for the back and seat of the chair, plus $1\frac{1}{2}$ in. on all edges for stretching and seam allowance.

Strong white cotton fabric for backing.

Anchor Tapisserie Wool in the following colours: white 0402; orange 0333; yellow 0298; dark green 0229; light green 0279; dark purple 0417; light purple 097; dark red 013; light red 0335.

Plastic foam cut to size and shape of cushions for padding.

A crewel needle No 18.

To make

Cut paper patterns in the size and shape to fit the chair back and seat. Place the patterns on to the canvas and mark the outlines with tacking stitches. Leave $1\frac{1}{2}$ in. spare all round each shape to allow for stretching and seam allowance. Work a line of tacking stitches both vertically and horizontally to mark the centre of each shape.

Starting from the centre and using two strands of yarn throughout, embroider the design in cross stitch (see Chapter 8) following chart (9). Each number on the chart represents a different colour. When all the work is completed stretch the canvas. Trim excess canvas to within $\frac{5}{8}$ in. of the embroidery. Cut a piece of backing fabric to the shape of the trimmed canvas for both back and seat.

Place the canvas and backing fabric together with right sides facing. Stitch all round $\frac{5}{8}$ in. from the edge, leaving an opening large enough to

9

insert the pad. Close opening with small oversewing stitches. Using white wool, embroider a row of cross stitches all round the edge of each cushion. At each of the four corners, using the wool double, make a chain in white to tie the cushions to the chair.

Key to chart

■ = white—0402	3 = dark green—0229	6 = light purple—097
1 = orange—0333	4 = light green—0279	7 = dark red—013
2 = yellow—0298	5 = dark purple—0417	8 = light red—0335

Squares and circles (See below, pages 57–58 and 157–9)

Simple shapes and bold, contrasting colours are used for these modern cushions embroidered in cross stitch. Grouped together they could provide an arresting block of colour against stark white walls. To make each of the cushions measuring approximately 16 in. square you will need:

A piece of double thread canvas, with 5 holes to 1 in., measuring 20 in. square.

Anchor Tapisserie Wool in the colours indicated on the chart.

Tweed fabric measuring 17 in. square for back of cushion.

Cushion pad measuring 18 in. square.

8 in. zip fastener.

To make the oblong cushion measuring approximately 12 in. by 24 in. you will need:

A piece of double thread canvas with 5 holes to 1 in. measuring 16 in. by 28 in.

Anchor Tapisserie Wool in the colours indicated on the chart.

Tweed fabric measuring 13 in. by 25 in. for back of cushion.

Cushion pad measuring 14 in. by 26 in.

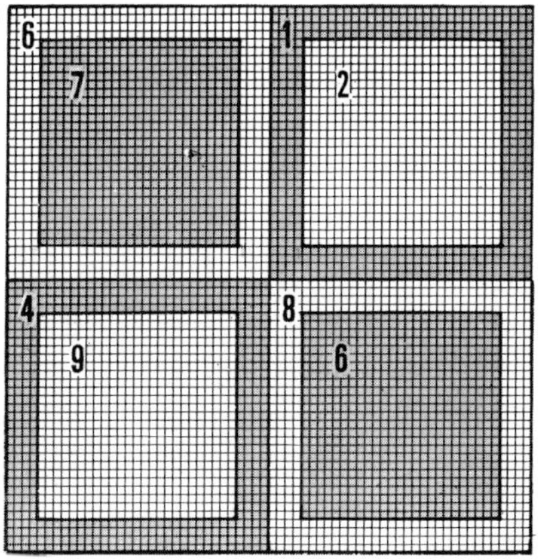

Colour key

1 = red—013
2 = light green—0238
3 = black—0403
4 = turquoise—0168
5 = blue—0148
6 = purple—0107
7 = orange—0332
8 = yellow—0298
9 = dark green—0205

(For enlargement, see page 157)

Rocking chair cushions (see pages 53–55)

Squares and circles (see page 55 and overleaf)

11
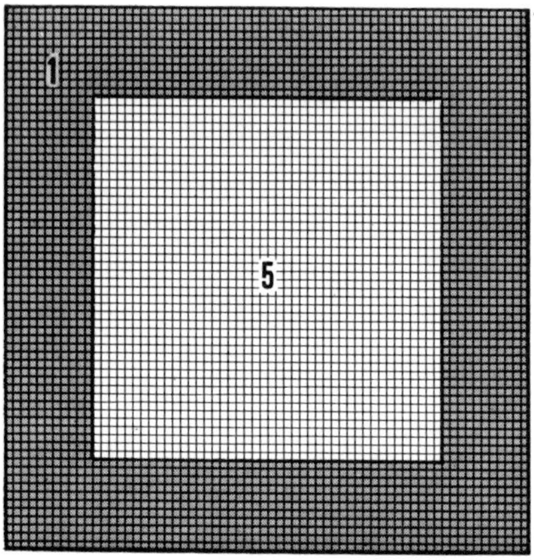

12
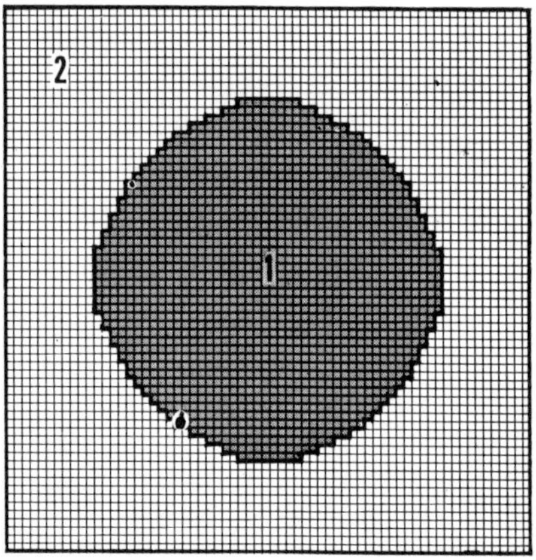

13
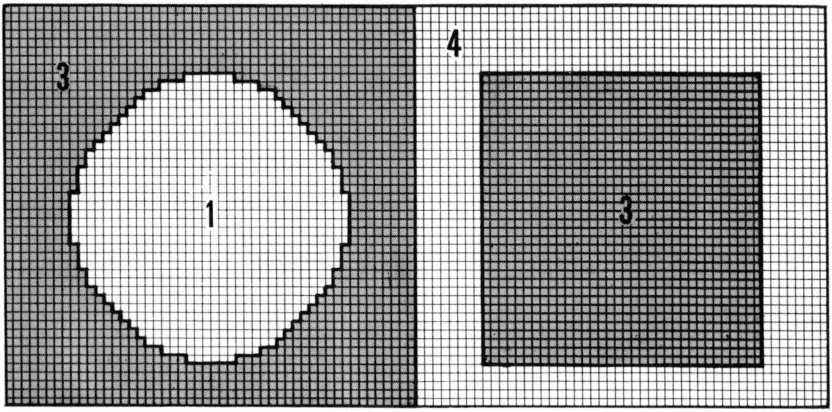

(For enlargements of these charts, see pages 158 and 159)

A 14 in. zip fastener for long side of cushion.

For both cushions you will need:

Black sewing cotton.

A tapestry needle No 18.

To work

Using the wool double throughout, embroider each cushion in cross stitch (see Chapter 8) following charts (10–13). Each square on the charts represents one cross stitch. When the work is complete stretch the canvas and trim back the excess to within four squares of canvas from the edge of the embroidery. Follow instructions given for making up a canvas work cushion in Chapter 7.

3 PATCHWORK

The ancient craft of patchwork is enjoying a revival of popularity and has taken on a lively new look in line with modern colour schemes. Patchwork can be successfully used in making all sorts of things from fashion garments such as dresses, skirts and jackets to furnishings for the home such as cushions, bedspreads, curtains and tea cosies.

The basic designs featured in this chapter can be adapted and used for making practically any item of patchwork. The designs can be enlarged or reduced by obtaining larger or smaller templates of the same shape to work with.

Equipment

Templates: These are used to make accurate patterns from which to cut the patches (see 1, overleaf). They are made of metal, perspex or stiff cardboard. The templates are cut to the exact size of the required patch, so allow about $\frac{3}{8}$ in. turnings round the edge of the template when cutting out a patch. Perspex or window templates are useful when working with patterned fabric as they make it possible to select the exact area of a pattern or motif required for each patch. There is a wide selection of templates in various shapes and sizes but hexagon templates in 1 in. or $1\frac{1}{2}$ in. sizes are the simplest shape to start working with. Diamond and square shapes tend to be a little more difficult to handle as they require great accuracy in sewing together.

Stiff paper: This is used to make the paper shapes for the patches over which the pieces of fabric are tacked. The best paper to use is that taken from glossy magazines. The papers must be accurately cut to ensure that the completed patchwork lies flat and unpuckered.

Cutting tools: The paper shapes are best cut using a special knife made for the purpose, although an old pair of scissors can be used. The advantage of using a knife is that the shapes are more likely to be accurate and several can be cut at one time. The cutting should be done over a piece of flat wood (an old bread board will do) or an old table protected by several layers of newspaper. A sharp pair of scissors is required to cut out the fabric patches.

Pins and needles: Fine steel pins are the best to use as these will not mark or leave holes in the fabric. If a very fine fabric such as silk is being used, pin the papers to the patches with fine sewing needles as these are even less likely to mark delicate fabrics. For the stitching, use Sharps needles in the finest size you can comfortably work with. The finer the needle, the smaller and neater are the resulting stitches.

Thread: Use fine cotton for stitching cotton or linen patches and pure silk for silk and velvet patches. For tacking the patches over the papers use mercerised sewing cotton such as SYLKO or a pure silk, as these are less likely to leave marks than tacking cotton. This is an important point as the tacking stitches remain in the fabric for some time and a coarse thread can leave marks which are almost impossible to remove.

Fabrics: Any odd scraps of fabric can be used, provided all the types used in one piece of work are of a similar weight. If you put a coarse cotton patch close to a fine lawn one it can pull it to shreds. If the completed article will require laundering, avoid mixing different types of fabric together. For example, if rayon and cotton are mixed, problems will arise in washing and ironing temperatures. Rayon requires a medium temperature wash and a cool iron whereas cotton requires a fairly hot iron which will scorch or even melt the rayon.

A firmly woven cotton is the easiest fabric to handle in patchwork. Avoid using very fine or slippery fabrics until you have had some practice in working with cotton. Velvet looks very effective in patchwork but it is one of the most difficult fabrics to handle and is best left until you are really experienced. Fabrics which fray easily are not really suitable. Before cutting the patches, always remember to press all creases out of the fabric.

Making the patches

Hold the template firmly on the paper and cut out the shapes carefully. If you prefer to draw round the template before cutting out, keep the pencil well sharpened and always hold it at the same angle. Cut the papers accurately through the centre of the pencil line.

Using the template as a guide, cut out the patches (see diagram 2) allow-

1

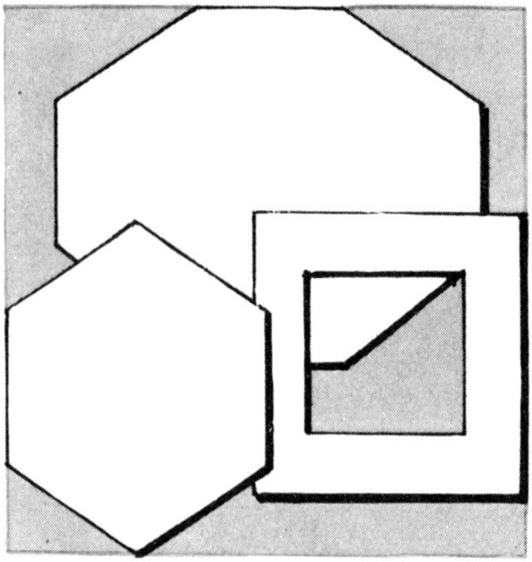

2

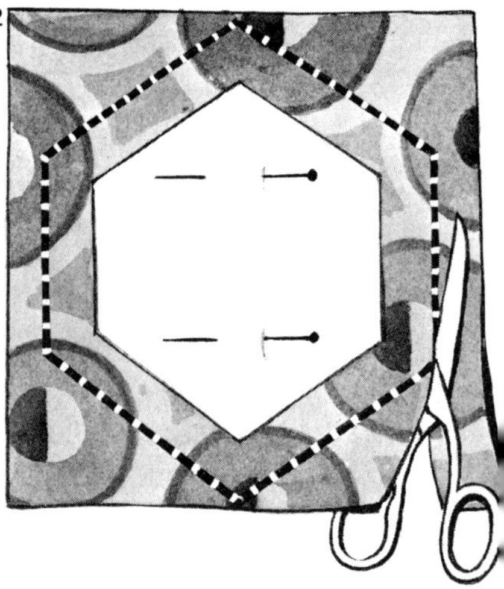

ing $\frac{3}{8}$ in. turnings on cotton and similar weight fabrics and slightly more on thicker fabrics. Place two edges of the template parallel to the grain of the fabric, whenever possible, as this produces a stronger patch. Pin the paper shape on to the wrong side of the fabric, fold over and tack the turnings accurately in place (see diagram 3). Starting with a back stitch or a knot, tack round the patch using one tacking stitch at each corner to hold it down. Finish off with a back stitch and remove the pin.

To check the accuracy of the patch, lay the template on to the right side of the patch. Both patch and template should be the same shape and size.

Joining them up: Place two patches together with right sides facing and join with tiny oversewing stitches along one edge (see diagram 4). Begin by laying the end of the thread along the top edge of the patch and stitch over it from left to right. Insert the needle into the fabric at right angles to ensure that the stitches will be small and neat. To fasten off, work backwards for four stitches.

You will find it much easier to handle the work in small sections. Stitch small groups of patches together at a time and when several groups have been made, join these together in a pleasing arrangement.

Finishing: When all the patchwork is completed, press it well on the back of the work over a damp cloth if necessary. If the front of the work requires pressing (see diagram 5), take out all the tacking stitches but leave the papers in until after pressing; this prevents an impression of the turnings coming through to the right side. Take out all the papers and keep the ones which are in good condition as these can be used again. From the right side of the patchwork tack the turnings all round the edge. To remove any marks left in the fabric by the tacking, press again on the wrong side. Good pressing is important at this stage as it 'sets' the work and helps it to keep its shape better when it is washed.

Mounting

The patchwork is now ready to be mounted on to a backing fabric or applied

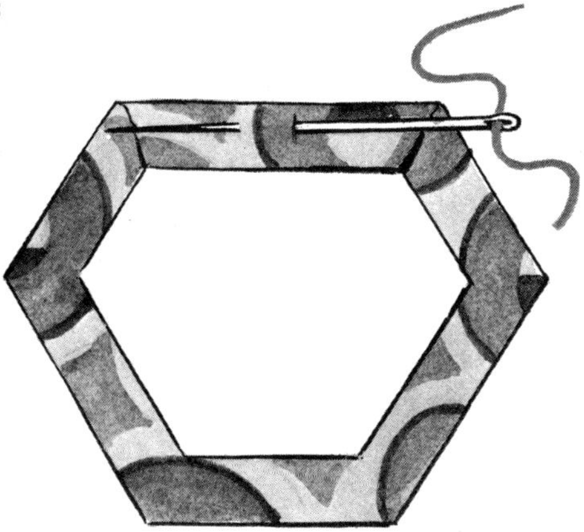

4

5

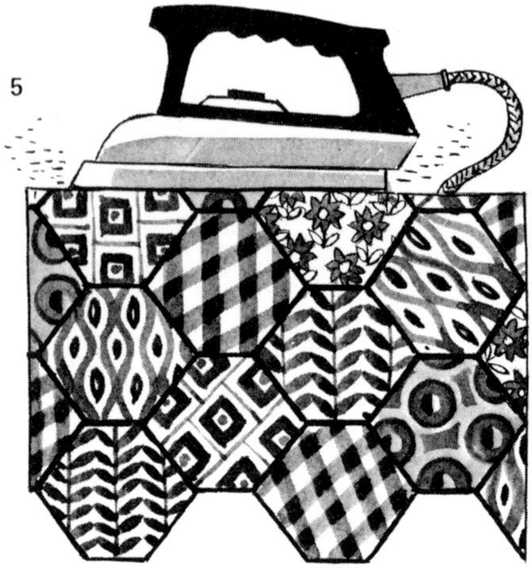

6

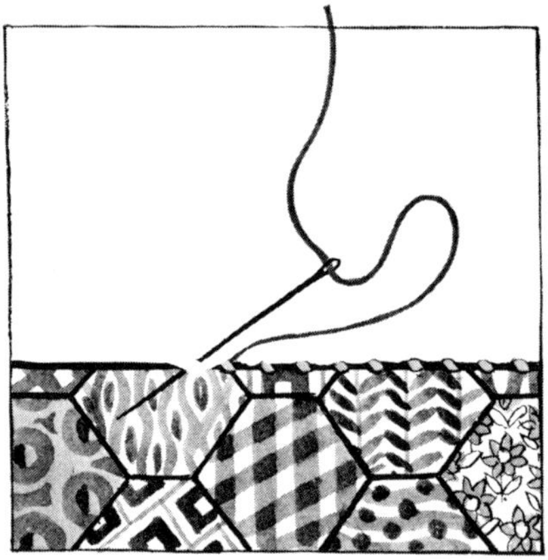

on to the article it is to decorate. If the work is being used as a form of decoration, tack it in place and secure it to the background fabric with tiny hemming or slip stitches (see diagram 6) then remove the tacking stitches and press on the wrong side.

If it is to be used on its own as a bed cover, for example, it should be mounted on pre-shrunk sheeting or calico. Pin and tack the patchwork on to the backing fabric, leaving the edges free. Turn in the edges all round, tack patchwork and backing edges together and slip stitch. If the piece of patchwork is quite large it should be attached to the backing fabric at 6 in. intervals at the corners of patches. Thread a needle with a length of cotton, bring the needle from the back of the work to the right side and back to the wrong side, taking a small stitch. Tie the ends at the back of the work into a reef knot and snip the ends fairly close to the knot.

A traditional finish to patchwork is to insert a piping all round the edge before joining the two layers together; this usually looks best if made from the darkest colour used in the patchwork. Another pretty finish is to make a frill from double fabric. The frill is attached to the patchwork and the backing fabric tacked and hemmed over the raw edges.

A clutch of cushions

These very attractive cushions are made using the basic patchwork shapes arranged in simple but eye-catching designs. A wide variety of different effects can be achieved by choice of fabrics and careful planning. To make up the cushions, see *Mounting* in this chapter and follow general instructions for cushion covers in Chapter 7.

Oblong patch (See below left and page 64)

To make this cushion measuring 18 in. square you will need:

A cardboard template cut $1\frac{1}{2}$ in. by 6 in.
A piece of fabric for backing cushion measuring $19\frac{1}{4}$ in. square.
A cushion pad measuring 20 in. square.
Scraps of fabric in 7 different colours.
Sewing cotton.
Sharps needle—fine.
A zip fastener measuring 12 in.

To work
Make the oblong patches up into nine squares of four patches each in four different colours, then join the squares together with the direction of the patches alternating. (See diagram 7.)

Tile patch (See below right and page 64)

To make this cushion measuring $14\frac{1}{4}$ in. square you will need:

Octagon template size $1\frac{1}{2}$ in.
Long hexagon template size $1\frac{1}{2}$ in.
Square template size $1\frac{1}{2}$ in.

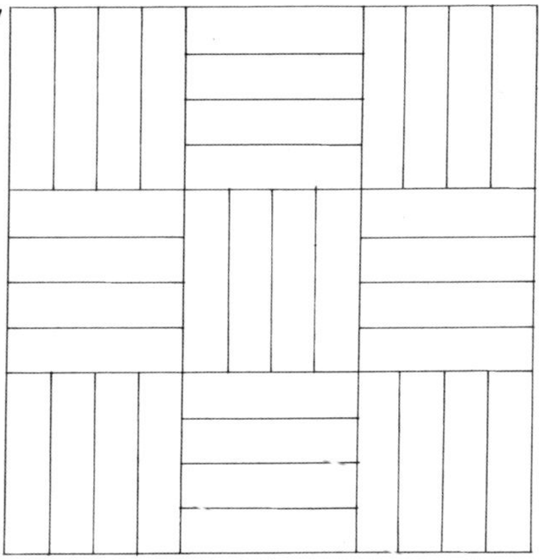

8

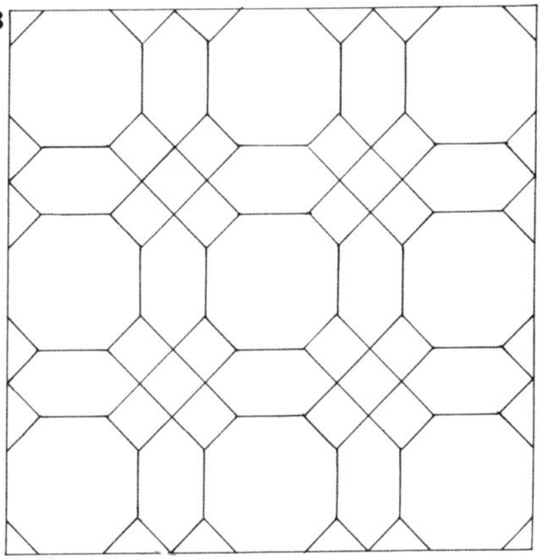

Above: *Oblong patch* (see previous page)

Below: *Tile patch* (see previous page and page 66)

Above: *Jackson star* (see overleaf)

Left: *Roman square* (see overleaf and page 67)

Scraps of fabric in light and dark checks, plain black and white.
A piece of fabric measuring 15½ in. square for backing cushion.
A cushion pad measuring 16 in. square.
A zip fastener measuring 10 in.
Sewing cotton.
Sharps needle—fine.

To work

Make up the centre design unit first, then continue working outwards, arranging the plain and printed fabrics as shown in picture. (See diagram 8.)

Jackson star (See below left and page 65)

To make this cushion measuring 14 in. square you will need:

Square template 2 in. size.
Diamond template 2 in. size.
Triangle template 2 in. size.
Scraps of fabric in red and white stripe, black with white dots and plain red, or an assortment of spots and stripes.
A piece of fabric measuring 15¼ in. square for backing cushion.
Cushion pad measuring 16 in. square.
A zip fastener measuring 10 in.
Sewing cotton.
Sharps needle—fine.

To work

First work the centre motif with the stripes radiating out, then complete the design, working outwards. (See diagram 9.)

9

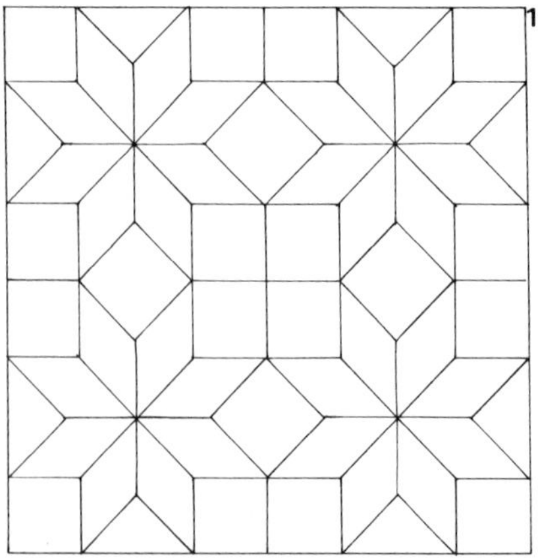

10

11

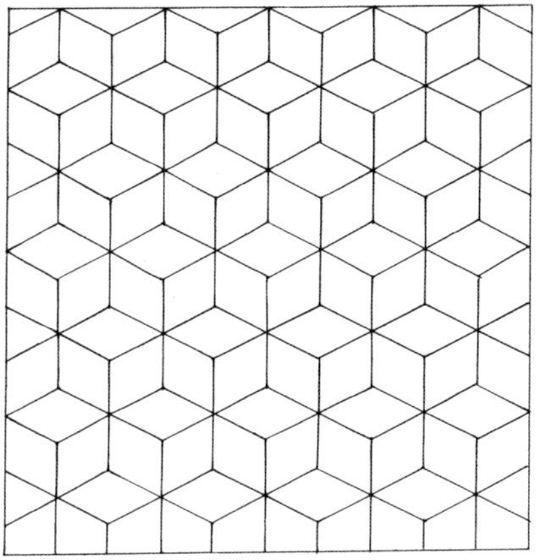

12

Roman square (See opposite and page 65)

To make this cushion measuring 19 in. square you will need:

Square template 2 in. size.
Scraps of fabric in four different prints.
A piece of fabric measuring $20\frac{1}{4}$ in. square for backing cushion.
Cushion pad measuring 20 in. square.
A zip fastener measuring 14 in.
Sewing cotton.
Sharps needle—fine.

To work
Work in diagonal rows from the centre outwards in both directions. Arrange the squares in a pattern selecting one for the border which is made up of squares halved diagonally into triangles. (See diagram 10.)

Building blocks (See above and page 68)

To make this cushion measuring 17 in. square you will need:

Diamond template 2 in. size.
Scraps of fabric in two contrasting colours and one toning print.
A piece of fabric measuring $18\frac{1}{4}$ in. square for back of cushion.
Sewing cotton.
Cushion pad measuring 18 in. square.
A zip fastener measuring 12 in.
Sewing cotton.
Sharps needle—fine.

Above: *Building blocks* (see previous and opposite pages)

Left: *Prairie star* (see opposite)

To work
Simply stitch diamonds into small, identical three-patch units before sewing all together. (See diagram 11.)

Prairie star (See page 67 and opposite)

To make this round cushion measuring 18 in. in diameter you will need:

Diamond template $1\frac{1}{4}$ in. size.
Scraps of plain and printed fabrics in five colours.
A plain cushion cover 18 in. in diameter.
A cushion pad measuring 18 in. in diameter.
Sewing cotton.
Sharps needle—fine.

To work
Begin the work from the centre and use eight diamonds of the same colour to form a star. Continue working in rows using one fabric for each row. Appliqué the completed star centrally on to the plain cushion cover. First tack star in place, then stitch with small hemming or slip stitches. (See diagram 12.)

Sweet dreams quilt (see overleaf)

Sweet dreams quilt (See previous page)

The simplicity of the design of this lovely patchwork quilt makes it equally suitable for a contemporary or a traditional setting. Choose a wide variety of prints containing a key colour, such as vivid pink. To make the quilt you will need:

Square template 3 in. size, cut in card.
A large selection of printed scraps of fabric.
A few ½ yd lengths of fabric for patches to sprinkle throughout for continuity.
A large sheet or some unbleached calico for backing (pre-shrunk).
Sewing cotton.
Sharps needle—fine.

To work

Prepare a large pile of patches with ½ in. turnings. Stitch the patches together in groups of nine, distributing the patterned fabrics evenly in each unit. To complete, join the nine patch units together to required size of quilt. Press and remove papers. Lay the completed patchwork over a large sheet or a backing of unbleached calico and smooth out carefully.

Pin the two layers of fabric together and work lines of tacking stitches in rows 6 in. apart. Secure the two layers of fabric together by making knots at the corner of patches at 6 in. intervals. Turn in the edges of the backing fabric all round to match patchwork. Slip-stitch patchwork and backing fabric together on all edges. Press and remove all tacking stitches.

4 APPLIQUE

The method of decoration known as appliqué is achieved by applying shapes of fabric and various materials to a fabric background. It is one of the oldest forms of decoration, dating from Greek and Roman times. In the Middle Ages it was used for depicting the crests of knights in armour on their banners or horses' trappings. Today, it is one of the most popular forms of decoration, used either on its own or embellished by the addition of embroidery stitches. It can be used to decorate many types of furnishings for the home and to give an individual touch to clothes.

Equipment

Needles: Fine crewel needles, the size depending on the thickness of the fabric being worked.

Thread: Mercerised sewing cotton such as SYLKO should be used for cotton fabrics; synthetic thread for man-made fabrics and pure silk sewing thread for silk fabrics.

Scissors: Two pairs of sharp scissors are required, one for cutting fabrics and a small pair for snipping thread and cutting close to the stitching on applied shapes.

Paper: If cutting a complicated shape, it will be necessary to make a template. Pages from glossy magazines are ideal for this.

Pins: To avoid leaving marks in the fabrics, use the best fine steel pins.

Thimble: A well-fitting steel or silver thimble is necessary to enable correct holding of the needle.

Frame: Most appliqué is best worked in an embroidery frame, as both the background fabric and the shapes to be applied should be stretched taut at an equal tension. Use a tambour frame for small pieces of work and a slate frame for larger pieces (for frames, see introduction to Chapter 1).

Fabrics

For appliqué, the applied fabrics should be either lighter than the background fabric or of equal weight. The background fabric can be mounted on calico or strong cotton to give added strength if required; mounting is particularly recommended for such things as wall hangings, pictures, curtains and bed covers and will greatly improve the finished appearance.

Fabrics which do not fray too quickly are the easiest to apply, as the edges need not be turned in. Felt or closely-woven cotton are the best fabrics to start off with as they are easy to handle. If you need to use a material which does fray quickly, iron on a woven adhesive interfacing to the wrong side of the fabric.

It is always advisable, if you want to be able to wash the finished article, to check the colour fastness of the fabrics by washing a small piece and ironing it while it is still wet over a piece of white fabric. If the dye in the fabric runs, it can ruin the whole piece of work.

Whenever possible, match the grain of the fabric to be applied to the grain of the background fabric. This prevents puckering and splitting. Materials such as leather, suede or felt do not have a grain so these can be applied in any position.

Methods of appliqué

There are several different methods of applying the fabrics to the background. The choice will depend on which fabrics you are going to use, the effect you wish to achieve and the purpose to which the article is to be put.

1 Stick and stitch: This is the simplest method of appliqué and it is recommended for articles such as pictures and wall hangings. It is not suitable for things which will require laundering. Simply cut out the shapes and stick them to the background using a fabric adhesive. Then secure the edges either by hand or machine stitching.

2 Cut and stitch: This method is generally used on firm, non-fraying materials such as felt, suede and leather. Cut out the required shape and tack it into position. Stitching by hand, secure the shape to the background fabric with buttonhole stitch, blanket stitch, slip stitch or by machine, using straight or zig-zag stitches. For items such as wall hangings or pictures, interesting effects can be achieved by deliberately choosing fabrics which fray; this gives a softer outline. Stitch the shape to the background with a straight stitch on the sewing machine a little in from the edge and then fray out the edges of the fabric.

3 Stitch and cut: This method can be used on fabrics which would fray badly if cut out before applying. Cut out a piece of fabric larger than the shape. Mark the outline of the shape required on to the right side of the fabric and tack it to the background. Buttonhole stitch by hand or work round the edge of the shape with zig-zag stitch on the sewing machine. Using a very sharp pair of scissors, trim off the surplus fabric as close as possible to the stitching.

4 Blind appliqué: Cut out each shape to be applied adding $\frac{1}{4}$ in. to $\frac{3}{8}$ in. turnings on all edges. Fold the turnings to the back and tack in place. Position the shape on to the background fabric, then pin and tack in place. Stitch the shape to the background, using small slip or hemming stitches. If the shape to be applied is complicated, first cut out a paper template. Tack the fabric over the template in the same way as for patchwork, press on the wrong side and remove the template before stitching the shape on to the background.

To work appliqué

Trace the design centrally on to the background fabric. If backing fabric is to be used, tack the background fabric to this and mount the work in a frame. Prepare the shapes to be applied according to the appliqué method being used. Pin and tack the shapes in position, making sure they are perfectly flat and matched to the grain of the background fabric. Stitch in place.

Use a tambour frame for small items, and if the shapes are to be applied by machine. If the work is mounted in the tambour frame for machine working it should be mounted with the right side of the background facing the wrong side of the frame, so that the fabric lies flat on the bed of the machine. Larger pieces of work should be mounted in a slate frame.

Still life in a blue bowl (See below and pages 74–76)

Capriciously-coloured fruit overflowing from its bowl makes an effective design for a picture, to be mounted simply in a gold frame. Make the picture any size you like and for an original design, rearrange the fruit as you please. You will need:

A piece of fabric for the background.
Scraps of fabric in assorted colours and textures.
Fabric adhesive.
Clark's Anchor Stranded Cotton in assorted colours (optional).

1

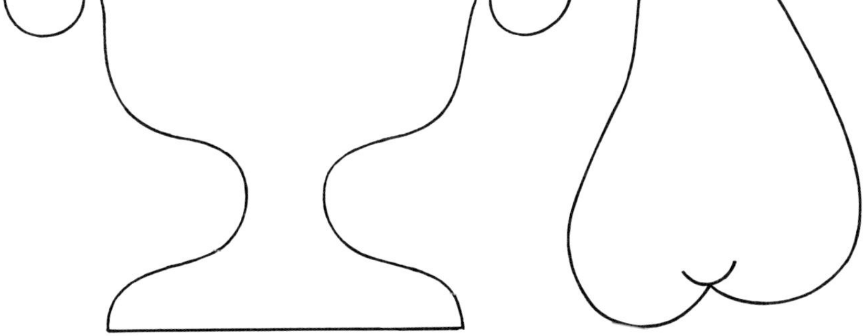

Hardboard for mounting.
A picture frame of the appropriate size.

To make

Trace and enlarge the outlines (1 and 2) to the required size (see Chapter 1 for enlarging). Transfer the shapes on to the back of the fabric to be applied and cut out four apples in different colours, three pears in different colours, two bunches of cherries, two plums and bowl. Place the shapes in the required arrangement on the background fabrics. The shapes in this picture have been merely stuck down on to the background fabric with adhesive but for a richer effect they can be outlined in embroidery stitches.

When the work is completed, press on the wrong side (omit if adhesive has been used) and mount over hardboard cut to required size and frame.

2

Lion window blind (See page 77)

This friendly lion motif has been used here very effectively to decorate a window blind for a child's room (several of the appliqué motifs in this chapter could be used for the same purpose). You will need:

A window blind of the required size.
Scraps of firm cotton fabric for the appliqué.
Ribbon to decorate hem.
Clark's Anchor Stranded Cotton to match fabric.

To work

Cut out the required shape (4) and tack in place in a central position on the window blind. Appliqué the shape to the background using buttonhole stitch (or any firm decorative stitch). Work the features and details in straight stitch and satin stitch (see Chapter 8) using three strands of cotton in the needle. Complete the decoration by stitching two lengths of ribbon spaced apart along the hem of the blind as shown.

Still life in a blue bowl (see pages 73–75)

4

Below: *Lion window blind* (see page 75); above: outline of the lion motif

Apple table cloth and matching lampshades (See page 80)

This cheerful set in bold appliqué carried out in brilliant colours would brighten a dark dining room in winter. It could be teamed with the *Apple Embroidered Cushion* in Chapter 1.

Apple table cloth

The cloth measures 78 in. by 70 in. You will need:

A piece of linen measuring 80 in. by 72 in. in red.
A piece of linen measuring 72 in. by 20 in. in yellow.
Small remnants of cotton fabric printed with small flowers.
Clark's Anchor Pearl Cotton No 5: 1 ball white 0402.
Sewing cotton: 1 spool red and 1 spool yellow to match linen.
A crewel needle No 7.

To work

Using the motif given for the apple cushion in Chapter 1 (11), trace and transfer it on to the yellow linen. There are three apples across the width of the panel and ten along the length. Make a narrow hem along each long side of the yellow panel and stitch by hand. Tack and stitch this panel down the centre of the red fabric. From the yellow panel cut out the left hand of each centre of the red fabric. From the yellow panel cut out the left half of each apple and the right half of the heart (being careful, of course, not to cut through the red fabric). From the remnants of flowered cotton, cut the right half for each motif. Pin the flowered sections on each apple and tack in place. Stitch down the edges of the printed sections with small satin stitch (see Chapter 8) in white Pearl Cotton. Continue working satin stitch all round the apple. Work the details such as stalks and leaves in satin stitch.

To secure the yellow fabric firmly to the background, work a line of machine stitches in matching yellow between each row of apples. Make a $\frac{1}{2}$ in. hem all round the cloth and mitre the corners (see Chapter 7). Work a line of zig-zag satin stitch all round the hem to cover stitching. Press on the wrong side over a damp cloth.

Note: Satin stitching may be done by machine, if available.

Apple lampshades

These drum-shaped lampshades, like the matching table cloth, are worked in bold appliqué and brilliant colours. For each lampshade you will need:

A pair of lampshade rings measuring 12 in. in diameter.
White gloss paint or clear varnish for painting rings.
Cotton tape for binding the rings.

White bonding parchment measuring $38\frac{1}{2}$ in. by 12 in.
A piece of yellow cotton fabric measuring 39 in. by 12 in.
A piece of red cotton fabric measuring 39 in. by 9 in.
Scraps of printed fabric for apple halves.
3 yds red braid trimming.
Fabric adhesive.
A crewel needle No 7.

To work the appliqué

On the piece of red fabric, turn and tack $\frac{1}{2}$ in. turnings on each long edge. Press on the wrong side and place the red fabric centrally on to the piece of yellow fabric. Tack and slip stitch the red fabric securely in place. Trace the apple design as given for the *Apple Cushion* in Chapter 1, and enlarge it to measure $8\frac{1}{2}$ in. across. Transfer the design placed centrally on the red fabric, 1 in. in from the right hand edge. Then transfer three more apple motifs, leaving 1 in. space between each one. For the appliqué and embroidery, follow the instructions as given for the *Apple table cloth* and when completed, press well on the wrong side.

To make the lampshade

First paint the rings. When the paint is thoroughly dry, bind them tightly with the tape, making sure to overlap the edges. Place the bonding parchment on a flat surface with the shiny side up. Place the wrong side of the fabric centrally on to the parchment, with the fabric extending $\frac{1}{2}$ in. at the left hand side; the right hand edges of fabric and bonding parchment should be even. Hold the fabric in position using paper clips or weights. Pass a moderately hot iron over the fabric to enable the parchment to adhere to the fabric. Turn back the $\frac{1}{2}$ in. margin at the left hand side and stick it to the parchment with adhesive. Pin the fabric-covered parchment in position around the rings.

Using tiny stitches and two strands of cotton in the needle, sew the edge to the top ring, starting at the unfinished short end and stopping about 2 in. from the neatened end. Stitch the lower ring in position in the same way. Overlap the neatened short end and stitch into position. Complete the sewing of the upper and lower edges. Complete the lampshade by stitching a length of braid over the join and then around the top and bottom of the lampshade, to cover the raw edges of the fabric.

Giant flower cushion (See pages 81–82)

Good design in furnishing can often be achieved simply by the use of a continuing theme of colour or pattern. In the picture on page 8 the striking flower motif on the printed curtains is appliquéd on to the cushions, linking them together. If you have a remnant over from a pair of boldly patterned

Above: *Apple table cloth and matching lampshades* (see pages 78–79)

curtains, you could cut out your own motif and appliqué it to a cushion.

However, if this giant flower motif in glowing colours takes your fancy, here are instructions for making our cushion, which measures 24 in. square. You will need:

Two pieces of linen measuring 25¼ in. square in white.
A piece of linen measuring 23 in. square in rich pink.
A small piece of linen in red.
Clark's Anchor Stranded Cotton: two skeins each of pink 068 and red 047.
Anchor Tapisserie Wool: 1 skein black 0403.
White sewing cotton.
A zip fastener measuring 18 in.
A cushion pad measuring 26 in. square.

Below: *Giant flower cushion* (see pages 79, above and page 82)

To work

Enlarge the diagram (5) to fit a 24 in. square on paper and transfer the two parts of the pattern to the fabrics, cutting the centre of the flower in red. Using tapestry wool embroider the area indicated with French knots (see Chapter 8) worked closely together. Cut out a flower from the pink fabric allowing $\frac{1}{4}$ in. turnings all round. Tack the red centre on to the flower. Using 6 strands of cotton in the needle, work short rows of chain stitch all round the edge, working through both layers of fabric. Keep the outer edge of the stitching even but make the inner edge irregular.

Press the work on the wrong side. Turn $\frac{1}{4}$ in. to the wrong side all round the flower and tack. Pin and tack the flower centrally on to one square of white fabric. Work chain stitch through all layers of fabric in the same way as for the centre of the flower. Press on the wrong side. Make up the cushion cover in the usual way (see Chapter 7).

5

Animal silhouettes (See below and pages 77, 84–85)

These attractive animal silhouettes can be used in several ways. Combine them in an exciting nursery wall hanging, as in the picture on page 84, or use them separately on cushions, curtains or bed covers. Reduced in size,

they would make a pretty appliqué decoration for children's clothes.

Yet another use for the designs is to enlarge the shapes and use them as patterns for simple stuffed toys. To make the wall hanging measuring 45 in. by 20 in. you will need:

Plain, heavy cotton fabric for background measuring 49 in. by 24 in.

Scraps of assorted plain and printed cotton fabrics for the animals.

Clark's Anchor Stranded Cotton in assorted colours, for stitching on shapes and embroidering details.

A piece of hardboard measuring 45 in. by 20 in. for mounting.

Fabric adhesive.

To work

Enlarge and transfer the shapes (6 and 7) on to the fabrics to be applied (see Chapter 1 for enlarging and transferring). Using the 'stick and stitch'

Below: *Animal silhouettes* (see previous and opposite pages, and page 77)

7

method of appliqué (see introduction to this chapter), apply the animals to the background fabric in the arrangement shown in the picture. When all the shapes have been applied complete the details on the faces using straight stitches for the whiskers and satin stitch for the eyes and nose (see Chapter 8 for stitches). When completed, mount over hardboard (see Chapter 7 for mounting).

Note: For the lion motif, use the one given in *Lion window blind* earlier in this chapter.

5 NEEDLE-MADE RUGS

Rug-making is a craft in which several members of the family can take part. It is most rewarding and satisfying to do, as the work grows quickly. A needle-made rug will last at least 20 years and when it starts to show signs of wear it is simple to repair, so that its life can be prolonged almost indefinitely. There are two types, those made with a flat stitch and those made with pile stitch, both resembling the woven and knotted carpets of the east.

Flat stitched rugs

The equipment and materials required for rug-making are simple but the very best quality available should be used. Second rate materials will produce second rate results.

Equipment

Needles: Carpet needles with blunt points and large eyes are used for the coarse canvas used in making needle-made rugs and tapestry needles for the finer canvas. The needle eye should be sufficiently large enough for the wool to slip through easily.

Scissors and thimble: A 6-in. pair of very sharp surgical scissors with one blunt and one sharp point is ideal. As in all types of embroidery, a thimble is essential.

Graph paper: Sheets of graph paper with 5, 8 or 10 squares to 1 in. are used for charting the designs.

Crayons: It is best to use pencil crayons for making the charts as these can be rubbed out if a mistake is made.

Materials

Canvas: Two types of canvas are used, double mesh and single mesh. Double mesh canvas has pairs of threads running across both warp and weft, enclosing large holes through which most of the stitches are worked. This type is made in cotton, with 4 or 5 holes to 1 in., or in linen, with 7, 8 or 10 holes to 1 in. Canvas with 5 holes to 1 in. (5s) is the best size mesh to start on. Single mesh canvas is usually made of closely-woven jute with 8 threads to 1 in. Each stitch is worked over two threads of the canvas. This gives 4 stitches to the inch.

Wools: Again, these must be of the best quality, both for satisfactory results and durability. A wool and cotton mixture is not suitable. 2-ply Axminster thrums or hanks are used for the coarser double mesh canvases and Brussels or worsted thrums or hanks, and crewel wool for the finer single mesh canvas. Thrums are lengths of wool left over from making woven carpets and are obtainable in plain colours. Allow 6–7 oz of thrums to each sq ft of canvas. Tapestry wool is not suitable for any type of rug-making as it is too soft and will wear badly.

Planning your own design

You can, of course, buy your rug design but it is much more fun to make one to your own design. The two easiest methods are to plan your design on graph paper, using each square to represent one stitch, or to cut out shapes in paper, arrange them on graph paper and mark the outlines with pencil. There are many sources of inspiration for designs, including rugs and woven tapestries in museums. Another idea is to work out an all-over pattern using large patchwork templates.

When designing your own rug there are some general points to be borne in mind. The proportions and depth of the border are of the greatest importance as this gives strength and provides a framework which holds the design together. The border should measure at least $\frac{1}{6}$ of the rug. For example, a rug measuring 27 in. across should have a border at each side measuring at least $4\frac{1}{2}$ in. When designing a rug which is not being made to fit in to a particular area, the general proportions are for the length to measure $1\frac{3}{4}$ times the width. Always remember when buying canvas to allow for the turnover at each end of the rug and at least $\frac{1}{4}$ yd extra for any alterations which occur when planning the design on to the canvas.

A border is often divided into sections with one part more important, edged on either side with smaller supporting borders. Some motif or part of the main design should, if possible, be included in the border as a unifying link.

Before starting to plan your design, remember that as the rug is to be used on the floor the design must show up clearly when viewed from varying heights and from different angles. The number of stitches to the in. will also affect the design: a more flowing and intricate design can be planned on a fine mesh canvas, whereas the same design would have an angular, stepped appearance on a coarse canvas. A rectangle is usually the most convenient shape for a rug, although if you have an area which is suitable for a square rug, this shape can look very effective. Unusual shapes such as half-moons are not suitable for needle-made rugs because they waste a considerable amount of canvas; they can only be used in one position and the problems of working a curved edge are practically insurmountable.

Your design need not necessarily have a border and you might, for instance, like to start on one formed completely of stripes. Stripes are the simplest form of design and worked in different widths and stitches in an effective colour scheme, they can be most striking. Don't forget that lengthwise stripes will make a rug look longer and widthways stripes will make it appear wider.

If you prefer the idea of a rug worked in one colour, you would be well advised to use a combination of two or more stitches as one stitch throughout is likely to produce an uninteresting result and is boring to work.

Making a working chart

It is usually only necessary to make a chart of half the rug design and this is done by counting the number of holes in the length and width of the canvas. Count out this number of squares on the paper and draw half the design. Mark the depth of the border lightly in pencil as this may have to be adjusted later. Plan the motifs on a separate sheet of graph paper and select parts of these to be included in the border. With a free flowing border it is often

1

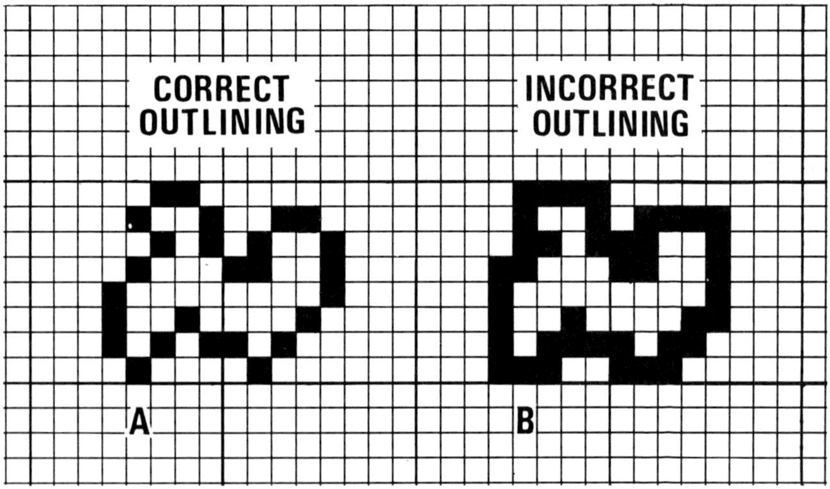

2

desirable to have a connecting motif at the corners. A corner is visually most important so this should be planned first. A small mirror will be found useful for selecting an area of design for the corner.

Outlining the motifs: This can add greatly to the general effect of a design. A motif can be outlined with one line of stitches or for a stronger effect a double outline can be worked. Never outline in black as this is too harsh (navy blue or dark brown are more effective) nor totally fill in the outline (see diagram 1).

Stitches

The stitches used for flat stitched rugs are the same as those used for canvas work, for example, cross stitch, double cross stitch, tent stitch (worked diagonally) instructions for which are given in Chapter 8. Soumak stitch and interlocking Gobelin stitch are also used. Back stitch is used mainly to fill the gaps between other stitches.

3

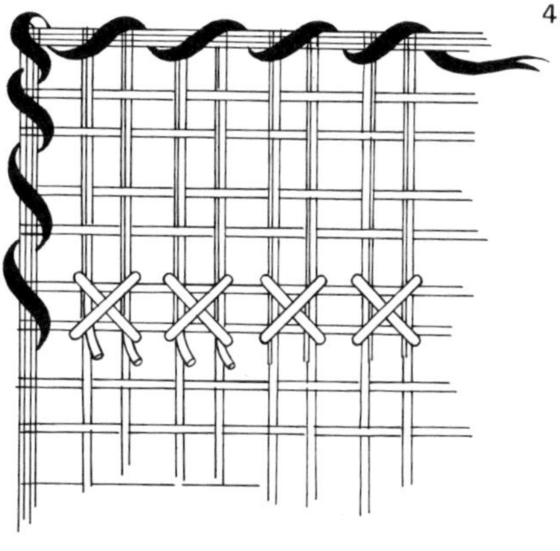

4a

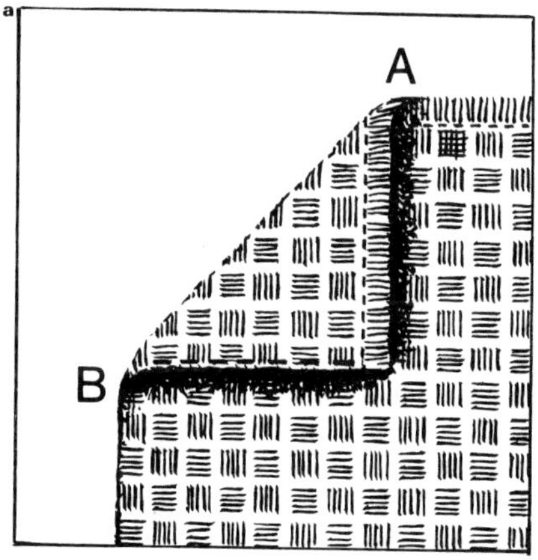

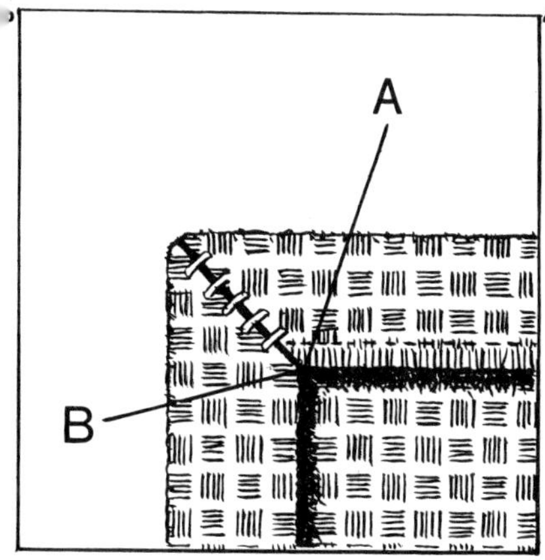

4c

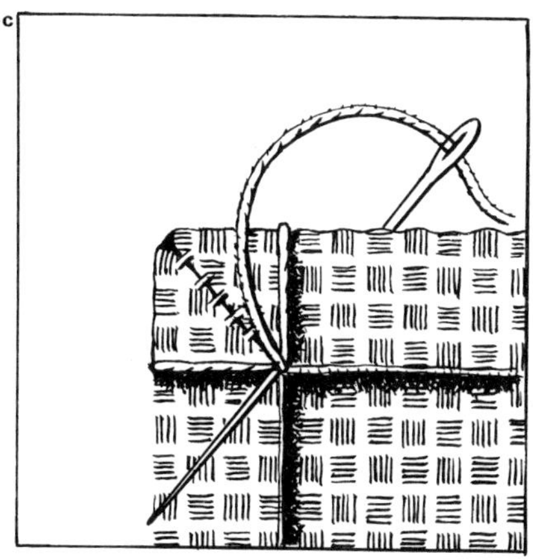

5

Preparation of canvas

Whatever type of canvas is being used, the cut edges must be dealt with before working the rug or they will fray badly. Turn the cut edges of the canvas over to the wrong side for flat stitched rugs and to the right side for tufted rugs. The turning should be 2–2½ in. for small rugs and a little more for larger ones.

With double mesh canvas, a double bar should lie along the folded edge to ensure that the large holes of the turned over canvas correspond precisely with those below (see diagram 2). Herringbone stitch the top raw edge firmly to the canvas using a complete cross stitch (diagram 3). The lower end of the canvas should be oversewn roughly along the cut edge to prevent fraying whilst working. If the side edges of the canvas are cut also, then they must be turned over to the same depth and the corners mitred. Do not cut excess canvas away; work through all thicknesses for added strength (diagrams 4a, b, c).

Edge stitching

The next important step is the edge stitching, which should completely cover the canvas. The strongest method is plait stitch for all types of canvas, but when working on single mesh jute there are two alternative methods, i.e., double crochet and blanket stitch. The stitches should be worked between every thread of canvas and about 3 or 4 threads of canvas deep. Before commencing the plait stitch work a row of oversewing with one thread in the needle along the edge taking a stitch into every hole of the canvas as shown.

Plait stitch

This stitch can be worked from left to right or from right to left (see diagram 5). To strengthen the shape of the rug it is worked from the top right corner to top left corner and down the left hand side of the rug, then from the top right corner down the right hand side of the rug and across the bottom. With the right side of the rug facing, bring the needle out at the top right hand corner immediately next to the selvedge and two holes down. (Leave about 3 in. of wool lying along the top edge where it will be covered with stitches.) Take the needle over the canvas and bring it up through the next hole to the left. Take the needle over the canvas and bring it up 3 holes to the left. Take the needle over and bring it up 2 holes back. Continue the plait always working 3 holes on and 2 back, until a corner is reached.

To join a new length of wool, bring the old wool out to the right side on a long 3 hole stitch and leave it loose. Thread the new one along the back of the worked plait for a short distance, bring the needle out at the same hole and continue the plait in the usual way. The tail of the old wool is carried along until covered with stitches. The join should be invisible.

Corners: The points of the corners are difficult to cover neatly and it is

6

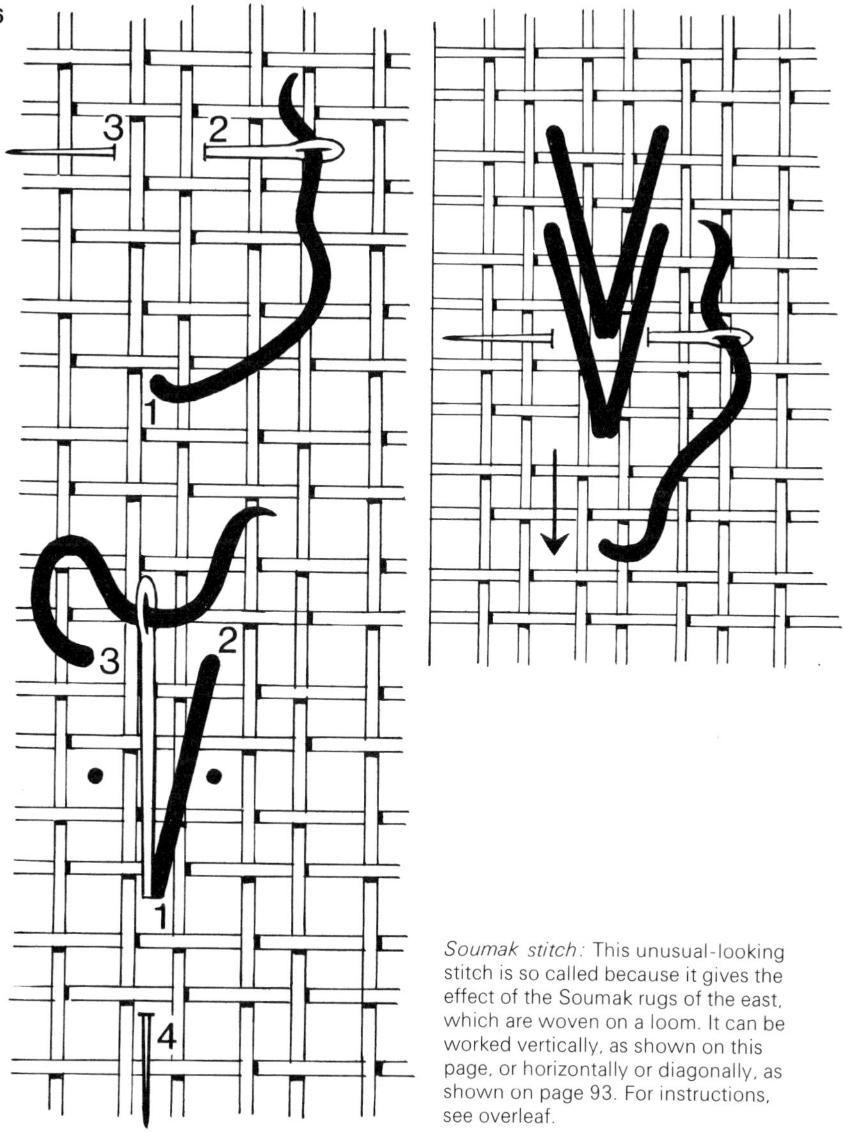

Soumak stitch: This unusual-looking stitch is so called because it gives the effect of the Soumak rugs of the east, which are woven on a loom. It can be worked vertically, as shown on this page, or horizontally or diagonally, as shown on page 93. For instructions, see overleaf.

helpful to paint them the same colour as the wool being used for the plait. When the paint is dry, work a single cross stitch over the point as an extra covering.

As the plait approaches the corner it should be shortened: when an 'on 3' stitch finishes in the corner hole it should be followed by back 2 on 2, back 1, on 1, so that the last stitch as well as the first along the edge is a simple cross stitch. Oversew the corner point neatly, covering the cross stitch already worked, and commence the plait down the selvedge as before with a cross stitch, the first half of which should be sloping in the direction in which the plait is to be worked. For pile rugs the edging stitch is always worked first but for flat-stitched rugs it is a matter of personal choice. If, for instance, the rug has to be stretched, it is often preferable to work the plait after stretching.

Fringes: With needle-made rugs, fringes are not really practical as they wear badly and can be a nuisance when vacuum cleaning. If particularly desired, however, a fringe may be worked as an alternative to the plait stitch as an edging. Finish the corners as described and then, using three or four strands of wool in the needle, work a row of Surrey stitch (see Rya type rugs later in this chapter) over the edge.

Soumak stitch

This is a most interesting, unusual-looking stitch which resembles the weave texture of the Soumak rugs of the east which are woven on a loom. The stitch is worked in vertical rows from top to bottom, or in horizontal rows from right to left or diagonally. The working position of the canvas differs from that used for any other type of needle-made rug. It must be held with the unworked length of canvas lying to the left and the V which each stitch forms is pointed towards the worker.

Vertical method: Using a single thread of yarn in the needle, commence each stitch at hole 1 between two threads of canvas (i.e., splitting the bar). Insert the needle up over two warp bars into hole 2, take it under a weft double bar from right to left into hole 3, and return the needle to the original starting point at hole 1. Drop the needle down between the threads of the next double bar to hole 4. The stitch is completed as before to form vertical rows (see diagrams 6 and 7).

Horizontal method: Working from right to left, insert the needle between the double bar to the left of the completed stitch instead of dropping down.

Diagonal method: For a diagonal line downwards from right to left, drop the needle down one bar diagonally each time. For a diagonal line upwards from right to left, move the needle up one bar diagonally. In each of these methods it should be remembered that each individual stitch should be worked and completed according to the basic method instructions.

When using Soumak stitch in rug-making it is necessary to work a row of back stitch between the first and last row of stitches and the edge stitches to avoid small gaps of canvas showing. The tension is important as it is easy to pull the stitches too tightly. When planning a design for this stitch allow one extra hole on the canvas than squares on the chart.

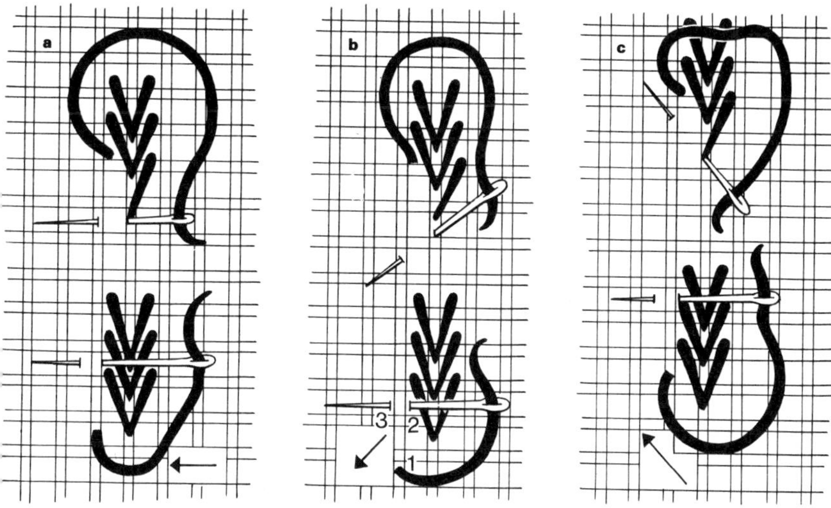

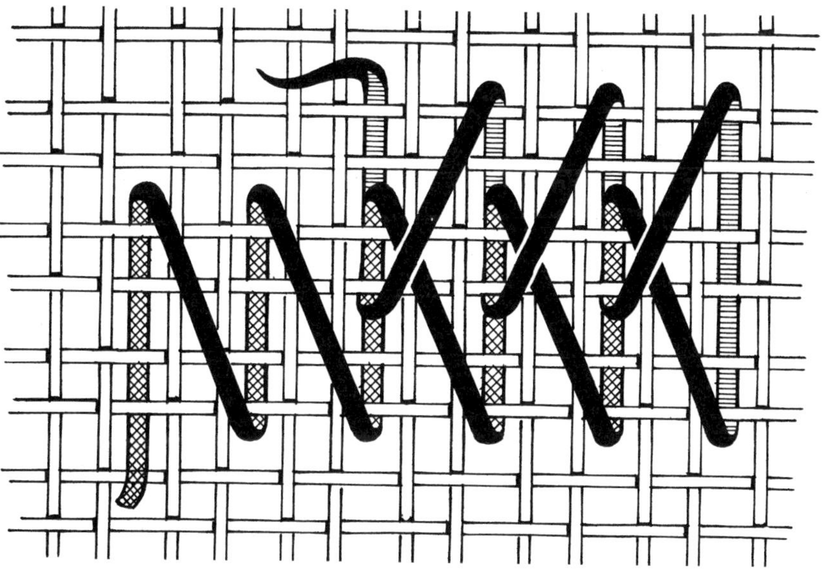

Interlocking Gobelin stitch

This stitch is quick and simple to do and is worked backwards and forwards in horizontal rows. It is particularly suitable for striped rugs and can be worked in horizontal or vertical stripes. Bring the needle out at top left, take it across 1 bar and insert it 2 holes down. Bring the needle out 2 holes up and continue to the end of the row. At the end of the row drop down an extra hole and work the second row in the opposite direction (see diagram 8).

Finishing

Most flat-stitched rugs are improved by stretching though it is rarely necessary to stretch a pile rug. Stretch the rug face down as for canvas work and dampen thoroughly. The rug should be left stretched for one week to allow it to dry completely. Brass nails should be used to prevent rusting.

Pile-stitched rugs

Pile-stitched rugs differ from the flat-stitched type in that they have a raised pile which can be shaggy and uneven (as in Rya type rugs), or smooth and velvety. The following are used in the making of pile-stitch rugs.

Surrey stitch

Diagram 9 shows clearly how to work this stitch in rows from left to right. As each stitch is completed pull the wool tightly to form a knot. To change colour, cut the end of the wool to the same length as the previous stitch and work the next stitch in the new colour. When each row is completed,

9

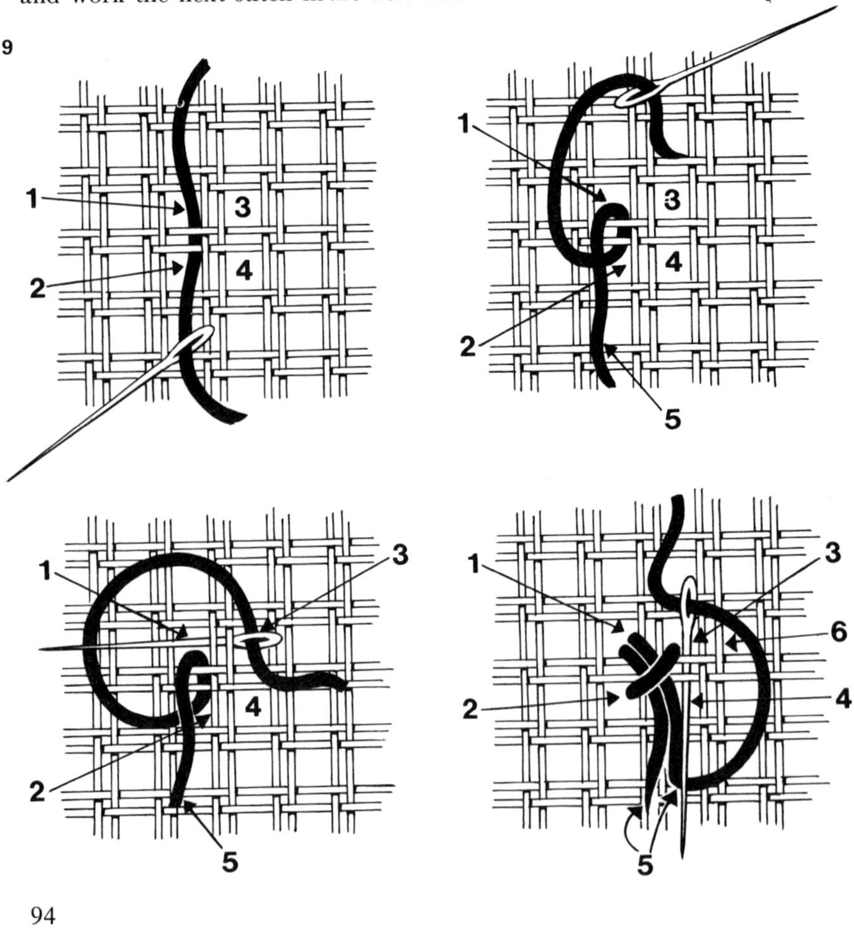

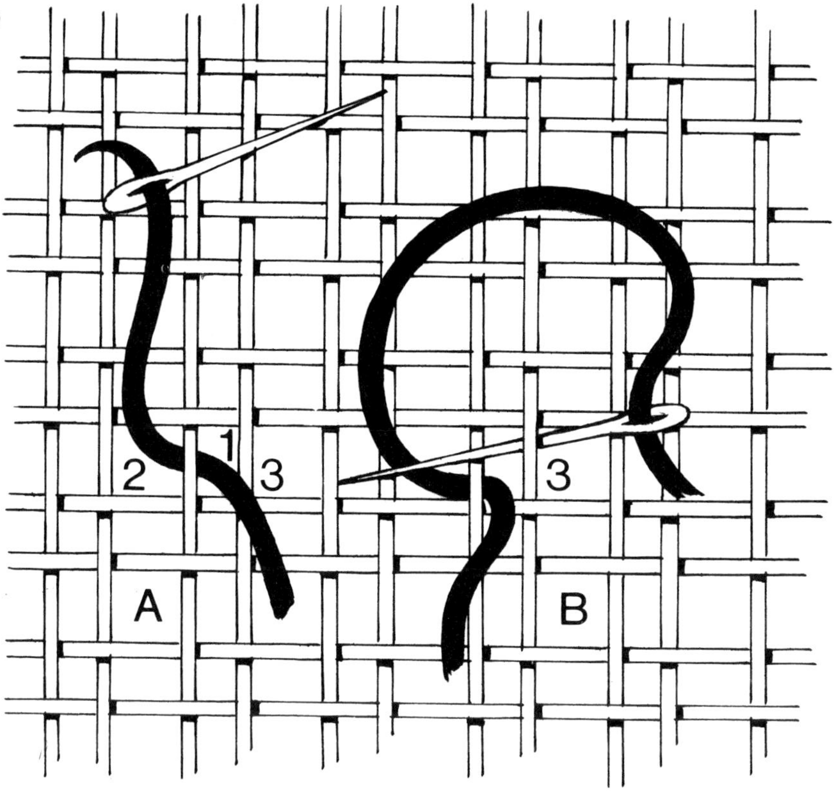

cut the loops, ensuring that all the ends are of an equal length. When the rug is completed, lay it flat on a table and trim the pile evenly all over to the required length.

Turkey or Ghiordes knot stitch

This stitch is worked in rows from left to right to form a pile similar to that of Surrey stitch and is adapted from the knot used in rug weaving. Colour changes are worked in the same way as for Surrey stitch. It is generally found that left-handed people prefer working this stitch to Surrey stitch (see diagrams 10 and 11).

Method of working

Work the plait stitch edging on a pile rug before commencing on the main part. For a firmer edge, a single row of long-legged cross stitch can be worked between the pile and the edge stitching.

A pile-stitched rug is commenced at the bottom left-hand corner and stitched in rows across the canvas from selvedge to selvedge and working away from the worker. As the stitched area of the rug grows, this should be rolled up out of the way. It is a good idea to roll the rug up over a sheet of

11

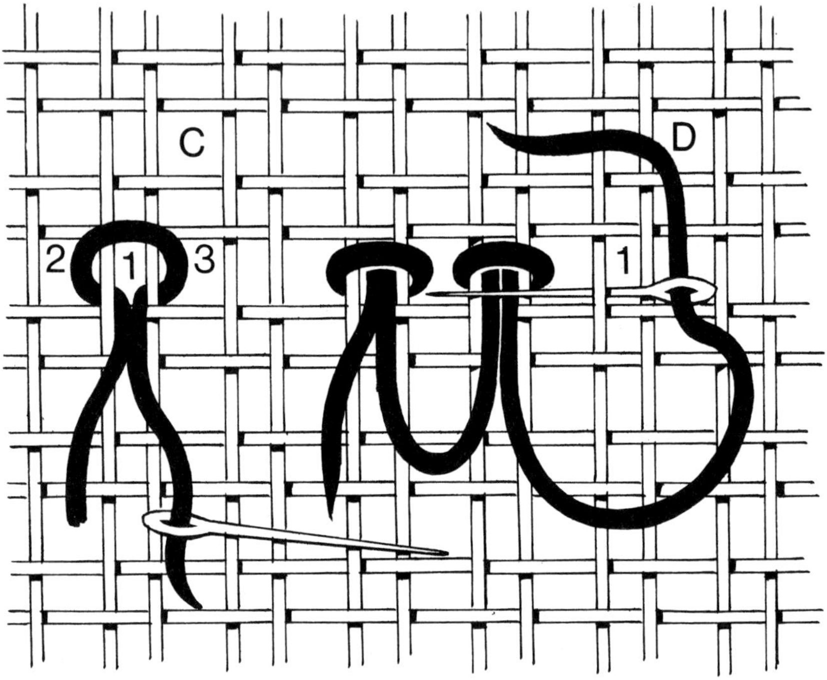

strong paper so that the stitching does not catch through the canvas into the worked pile. Do not change the working direction of the stitching as the pile will lie in different directions.

Rya type rugs

This type of needle-made rug is adapted from the Scandinavian loom-woven rugs; it takes the name Rya from a word meaning 'shaggy'. The designs are usually abstract and the rows of pile stitching are separated by rows of flat stitches. Only the pile rows of the designs are charted.

Materials

This type of rug is worked on a foundation of double mesh canvas with 4 holes to 1 in. The wool used is 2-ply Axminster thrums; 4 strands in the needle for the pile stitch and 3 strands in the needle for the separating rows of flat stitch.

Method of working

Each row of Surrey stitch (the pile stitch) is separated by rows of deep, long-legged cross stitch (worked over 2 bars instead of 1). For a 2-in. pile work three rows of the latter stitch; for a $2\frac{1}{2}$ in. pile rug work four rows. Work the rows of deep, long-legged cross stitch in opposite directions to prevent pulling the canvas out of shape. Work long-legged cross stitch over 4 holes of the canvas at each end of every pile row to prevent the pile of the rug hanging over the edges. The cut pile of the first row should reach just to the edge of the rug. When the final pile row has been completed, work one row of long-legged cross stitch. All the flat stitch background can, if preferred, be worked before commencing the pile stitching. The flat stitching is usually worked in the darkest colour being used in the design.

Yarn quantities for pile rugs

Use Axminster 2-ply thrums double on 5s canvas; Brussels wool double on 7s canvas and Brussels wool single on 10s canvas. Rya type rugs require 10–12 oz per sq. ft. Surrey stitch and Turkey knot stitch rugs use the same quantities as given for flat stitch rugs.

As personal working stitch tensions vary, it is always advisable to calculate a little over the quantity than under as dye lots vary considerably.

Cross stitch rug (see overleaf and page 99)

Cross stitch rug (See previous page, below and opposite)

This modern rug in striking colours and a bold, simple design is in quickly-worked cross stitch. This is a flat stitch rug but the same design can be used to work a pile rug. The rug measures 96 in. square. You will need:

11 yds of 27-in. wide canvas, with 3 holes to 1 in., cut and joined into a piece measuring 100 in. square.

Rug wool: 2½ lb in each of the following colours—white, black, grey and yellow.

Rug needle.

To work

Embroider the canvas in cross stitch, working two kinds of squares (see diagrams 12–13). The first is composed of several squares in different colour permutations. The second is also made of squares but has a diamond shape in the centre. To complete the rug work 36 squares (six rows of six squares in each). For placing the colours follow charts 1 and 2.

Chart 1 (below left)

There are 7 variations for arranging the colours:

A on chart: the part marked **1** will be in black, **2** grey, **3** yellow, **4** grey, **5** black.

B on chart: part **1** in grey	**2** black	**3** yellow	**4** black	**5** yellow
C on chart: part **1** in black	**2** yellow	**3** grey	**4** black	**5** yellow
D on chart: part **1** in yellow	**2** grey	**3** black	**4** yellow	**5** grey
E on chart: part **1** in yellow	**2** black	**3** yellow	**4** grey	**5** black
F on chart: part **1** in grey	**2** black	**3** yellow	**4** grey	**5** black
P on chart: part **1** in grey	**2** yellow	**3** grey	**4** black	**5** yellow

12

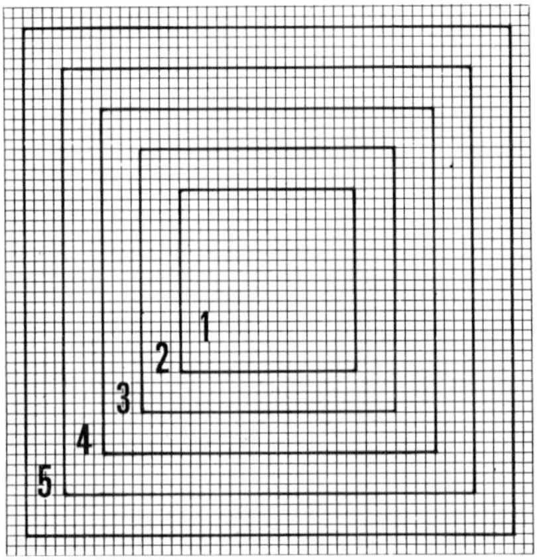

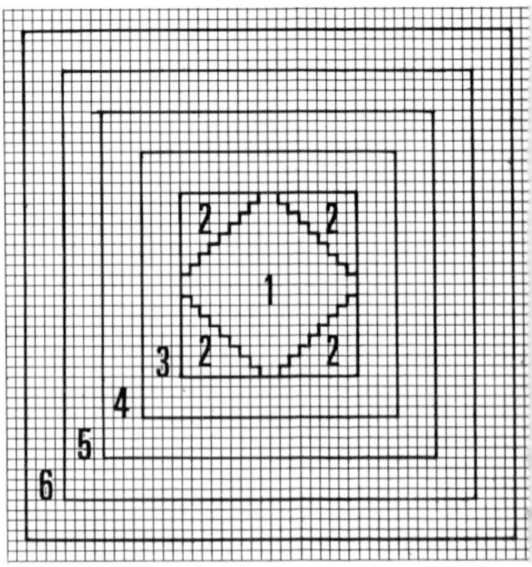

Chart 2 (opposite right)
There are 5 variations for arranging the colours:
G on chart: part marked **1** will be in black, **2** white, **3** grey, **4** yellow, **5** black, **6** grey.

L on chart: part **1** in black	**2** white	**3** yellow	**4** grey	**5** yellow	**6** black
M on chart: part **1** in yellow	**2** white	**3** black	**4** grey	**5** yellow	**6** black
N on chart: part **1** in grey	**2** white	**3** yellow	**4** grey	**5** black	**6** yellow
O on chart: part **1** in grey	**2** white	**3** black	**4** yellow	**5** grey	**6** black

To work
Mark a 96 in. square on the canvas with lines of tacking stitches. Turn and tack excess canvas to back, mitring the corners (see Chapter 7). Trim to within 2 in. of the outer edge.

If preferred each square may be worked separately and all 36 joined together when they are completed. If this method is used you will need 36 pieces of canvas measuring 19 in. square. Turn back $1\frac{1}{4}$ in. hem on all sides of each square and mitre the corners. Work each square individually. Then using black wool join them together with oversewing stitches.

Cross stitch rug: Left: The two patterns which make up this design; right: diagram showing half rug layout

A	G	L
B	M	N
G	C	D
L	E	P
D	L	M
F	O	L

6 SMOCKING

Smocking is an old English craft which has undergone a revival of popularity in recent years, being much favoured by fashion designers. The traditional farm labourer's smock was a thoroughly practical garment for the smocking was not only decorative but served the purpose of holding the fullness of the fabric in small pleats which made the smocked areas shower and windproof. It was usually worked on plain, coarse, evenly-woven linens and the gathering threads worked over the counted thread of the fabric. Today, smocking is worked on a wide variety of finer fabrics, checks, stripes and printed fabrics.

Remember that if you want to use smocking in dressmaking, the smocking should be completed before the garment is sewn together. It is not possible to smock ready-made garments, although you can decorate a garment with an inset of smocking worked on a separate piece of fabric.

Fabrics

The best fabrics to use for smocking are those of a smooth and even texture, such as cotton, silk, VIYELLA, or fine woollens. Fine fabrics such as voile and lawn look exquisite smocked but they require a little more practice in handling. Thicker fabrics are not suitable.

Estimating the quantity: The fabric before smocking should measure about three times the required finished width but this depends on the spaces between the dots, the firmness of the particular stitches used, and the individual working tension which varies from one person to another.

Yarns

Coton à broder or Pearl Cotton are the best yarns to use for smocking. Stranded yarns should not be used as they are not strong enough and are inclined to twist.

Smocking transfers

Smocking pleats must be even and transfers for planning the gathering dots are invaluable. Several different gauges are available. Dots printed close together make small pleats and are suitable for fine fabrics, while those

Flowery smocked nightdress (see pages 102–106)

which are widely spaced give a deep pleat and are better for heavier fabrics. Transfers with dots printed about $\frac{1}{4}$ in. apart are suitable for most fabrics.

Preparation for smocking

Cut the transfer to the depth and length required and iron it on to the wrong side of the fabric. Beginning at the first right hand dot, on the top line and on the wrong side of the fabric, secure the thread firmly with a knot and a back stitch. Working from right to left, carefully pick up each dot along the line leaving a few inches of the thread hanging loose at the end of the row. Repeat the process until all the rows are completed. Draw up all the gathering threads together, not too tightly (if you smock loosely, pull them a little tighter and if you smock tightly, loosen them a little). Knot the ends of the threads together in pairs and cut the threads to within 2 in. of the knots. Leave the gathering threads in place and remove them only when all the smocking has been completed. The gathering threads act as a guide to keep the smocking stitches straight whilst working.

Smocking on patterned fabrics: Spotted, striped or checked fabrics with an even pattern do not necessarily require gathering transfers but it is important to decide which area of the pattern is required on the surface of the finished smocking.

On spotted fabrics: Pick up each spot as if a transfer were being used. On subsequent rows, use spots directly under those in the first row or pick up a stitch immediately under a spot.

On striped fabrics: Mark rows of guide dots on the wrong side of the fabric with a pencil. The dot should be placed in the centre of a light stripe if the smocking is going to appear on a dark area and in the centre of a dark stripe if a light background to the smocking is desired.

On checked fabrics: Pick up the centre threads of the palest squares for a dark background to the smocking and pick up the centre threads to the darkest squares for a light background.

Flowery smocked nightdress (See pages 101–6)

This pretty nightdress is fitted and decorated with bands of smocking worked across the front and back bodice and at the top and wrist of the sleeves. The smocking is in colours picked out from the print of the fabric. The same pattern made up in a fine silk would look equally attractive as a dress. The nightdress pattern allows for 2 sizes, to fit either a 32 in. to 34 in., or a 36-in. bust. You will need:

$4\frac{1}{2}$ yds (for all sizes) 36 in. wide fabric without nap.

Clark's Anchor Coton à Broder in required colours (2 strands are used in the needle throughout).

Sewing cotton to match fabric.

Smocking transfer with $\frac{1}{4}$ in. spaced dots.

Graph paper for cutting pattern.

1

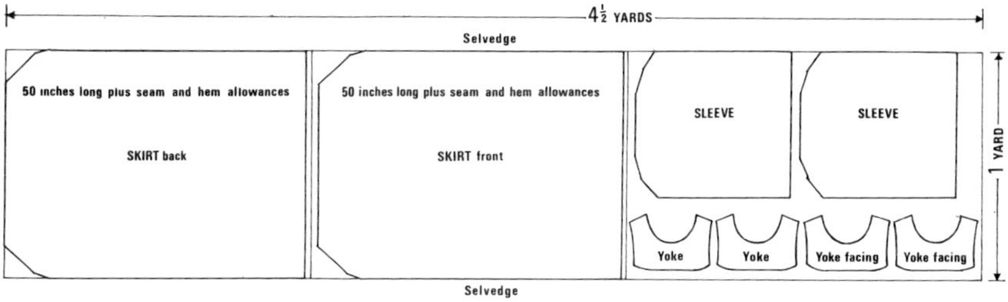

1 a

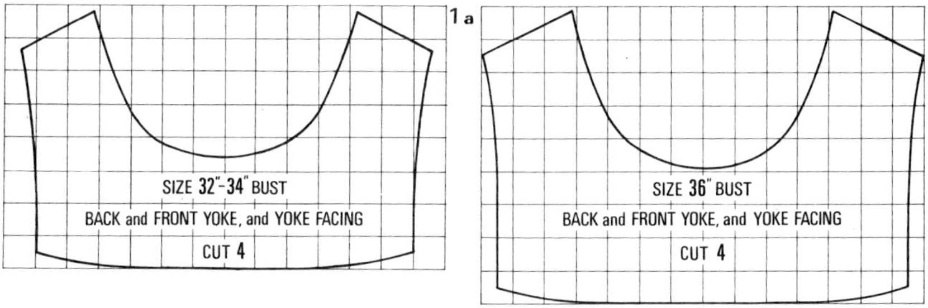

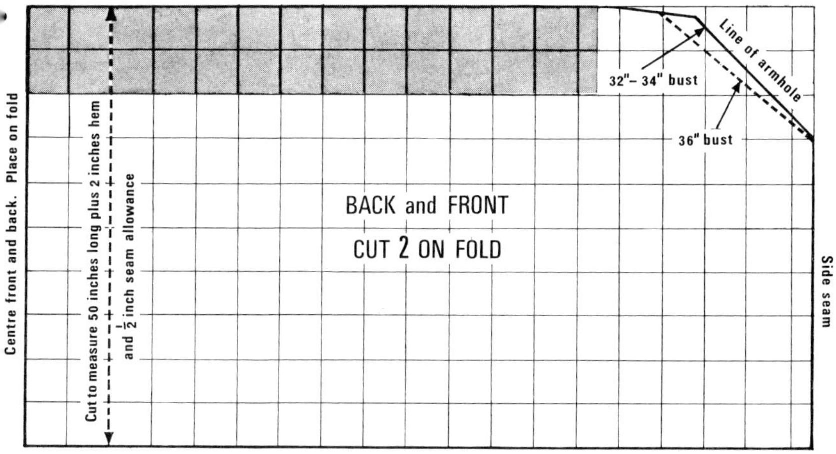

To make the pattern

There are three basic pattern pieces as follows:

Back and front yoke (bust size 36 in.) to be faced; cut 4. (Pattern for bust size 32 in. to 34 in. included.)

Back and front skirt; cut 2 on fold of fabric.

Sleeve; cut 2.

Make a pattern for pieces shown on the graphs (1a, b, c). Each square on the graph is 1 sq. in. There are no seam allowances included in the pattern so remember to add ½ in. to all seam edges and 2 in. at hem when cutting out.

This smocked nightdress design would also make a pretty dress

Smocking

The shaded areas on the pattern are to be smocked in the following stitches (see below): ROW 1, outline; ROW 2, cable; ROW 3, crossed diamond; ROW 4, outline; ROW 5, cable; ROWS 6, 7 and 8, crossed diamond; ROW 9, cable; ROW 10, outline; ROW 11, crossed diamond; ROW 12, cable; ROW 13, outline.

To make up

At either end of the smocking on the back and front skirt and the top of the sleeves, make a small tuck to enclose the uneven ends.

1 With right sides together, stitch front and back yokes together at shoulders and repeat this process with yoke facing. Press the seams open.

2 With right sides facing, stitch yoke facing to yoke round neck edge. Turn the yoke facing to back of work and tack round neckline.

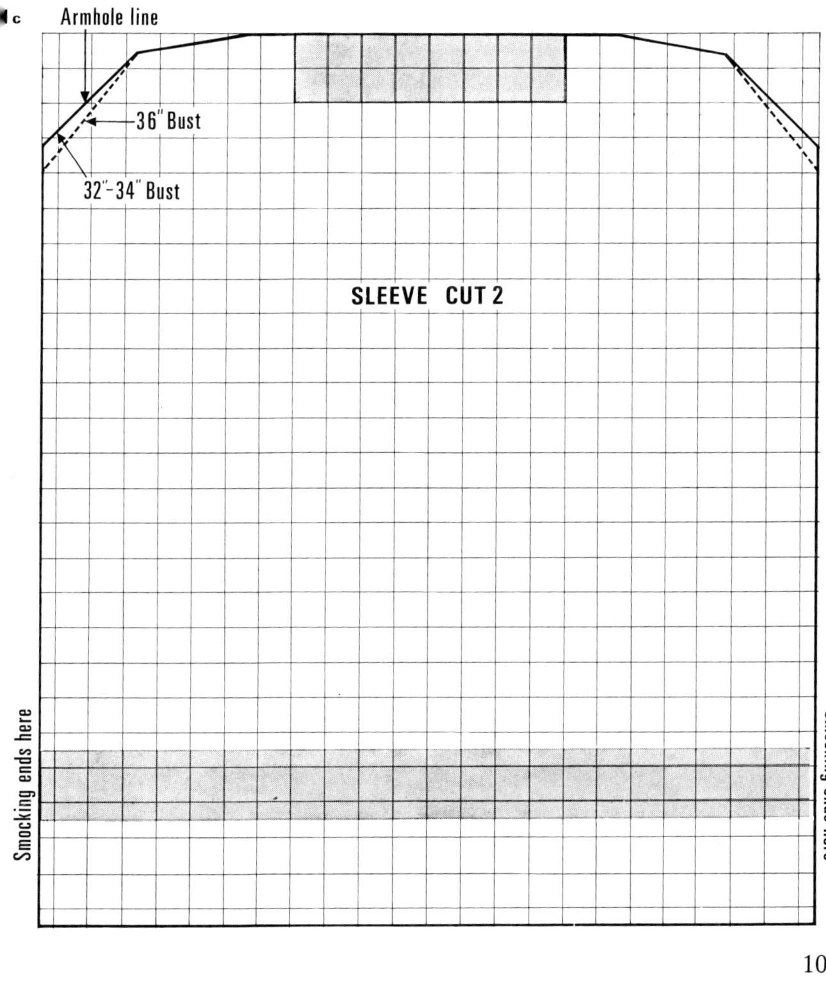

3 With right sides together, stitch the yoke to the back and front of the skirt. Press seam. With right sides together, stitch the yoke to the sleeves. Press seam.

4 Tack a ½ in. turning to the wrong side of the yoke facing on all raw edges. Press.

5 With right sides together, stitch the underarm seams.

6 With right sides together, stitch the sleeve and side seam of the gown. Press seams open.

7 Hem stitch the yoke facing on all edges to the machine stitching on the wrong side of the garment.

8 Make a narrow hem on the sleeve edge and a 1½ in. hem on the skirt of the gown.

Smocking stitches

Outline stitch

This stitch is similar to ordinary stem stitch; each stitch picks up one tube of the fabric. Outline is a firm-control stitch and two rows worked closely together at the top or base of the smocking will hold the pleats firmly in place. (Diagram 2.)

Cable stitch

This is also a firm-control stitch and two rows worked closely together at the top and base of a band of smocking prevent the work from fanning or spreading out. Cable stitch can be used as a single line or in several rows, worked closely together between rows of other smocking stitches. (Diagram 3.)

Trellis stitch

This stitch is worked in zig-zag lines. It is a loose-control stitch and could be used for the last line of smocking where a flare is required. (Diagram 4.)

3

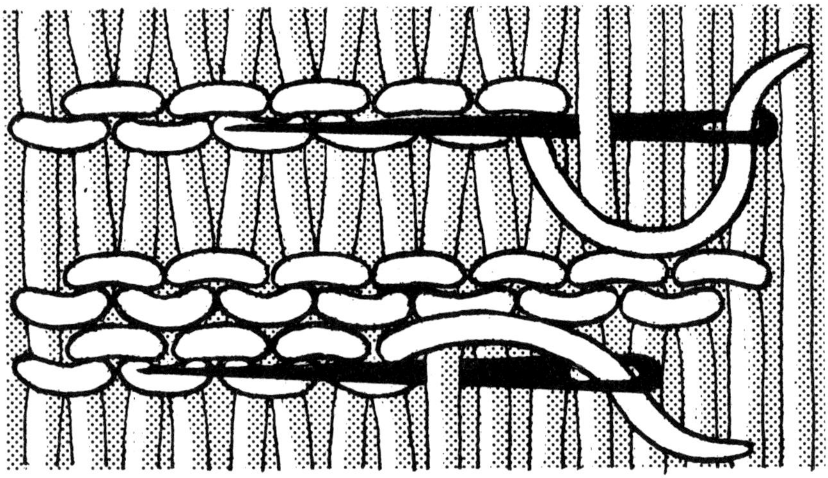

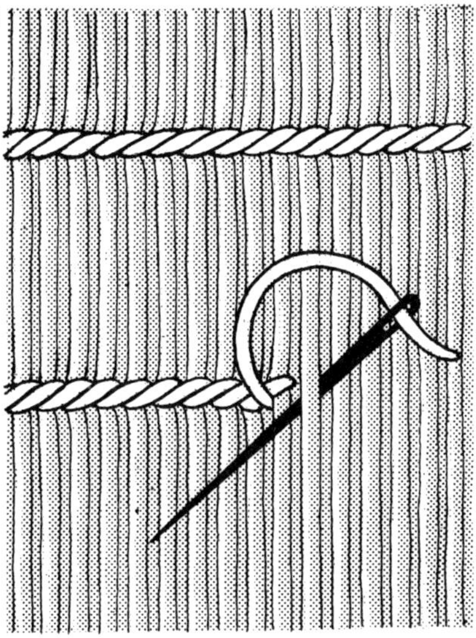

4

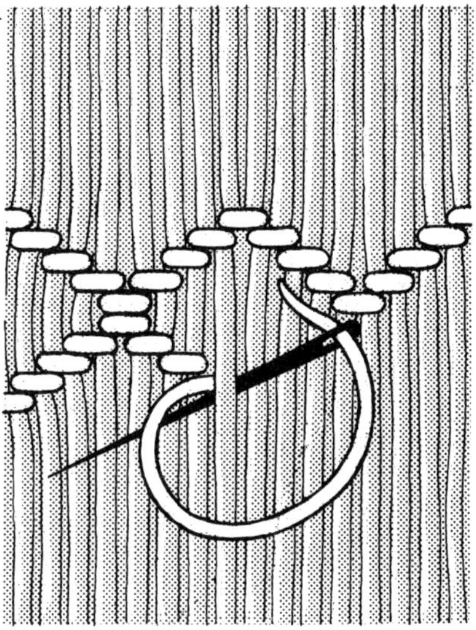

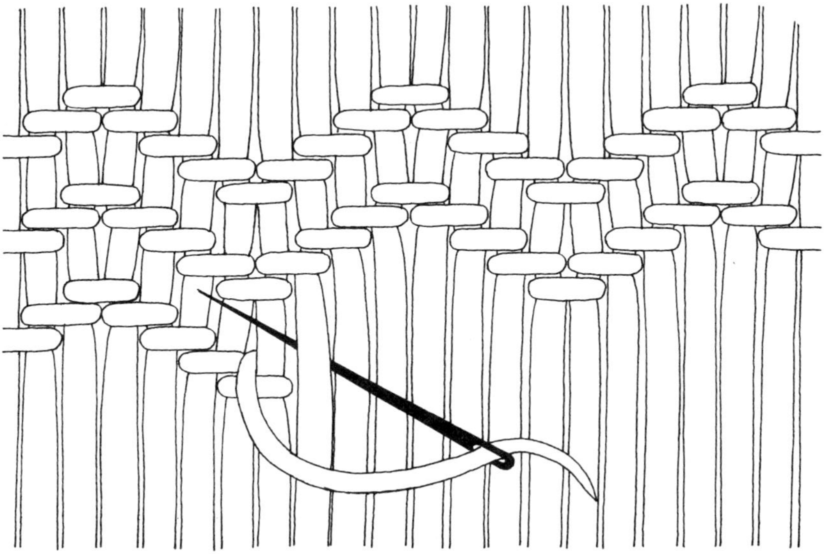

Wave stitch

This stitch is worked from left to right in a similar way to trellis stitch. As the upward steps are being worked, the thread lies below the needle; when working the downward steps, it lies above the needle. The second row is worked immediately below the first. (Diagram 5.)

Diamond stitch

This is one of the larger smocking stitches and care should be taken not to work it too large or the finished smocking will be slack. The stitch is worked from left to right in two stages and each stage is worked between two rows of gathering threads. If the gathering threads are spaced $\frac{1}{4}$ in. apart, the complete depth of the stitch will be $\frac{1}{2}$ in. (Diagrams 6a and b.)

Crossed diamond stitch

This is worked in the same way as ordinary diamond stitch but a second row is worked on top of the first, picking up the free pleats between the stitches on the first row. This second row of stitching can be worked in a self or contrasting colour. (Diagram 7.)

6a

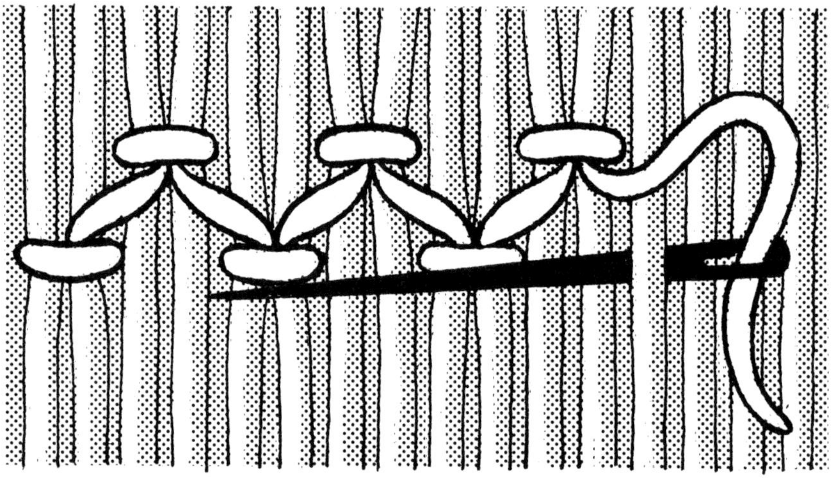

6b

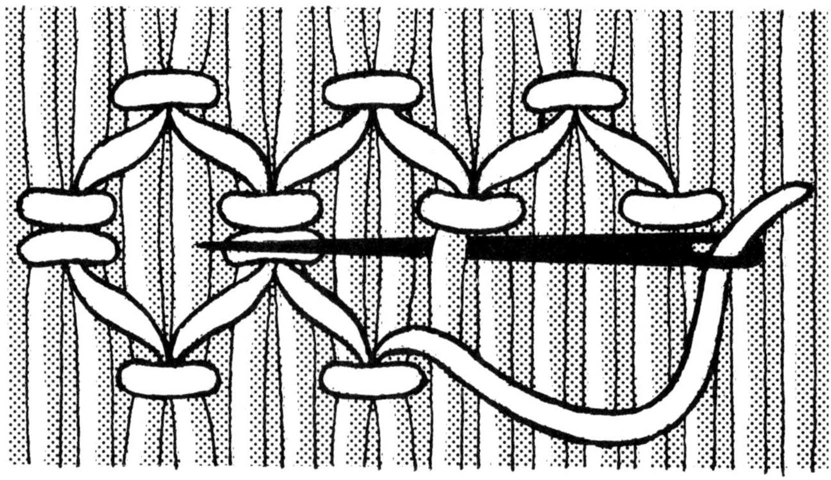

Vandyke stitch

Vandyke stitch is a small firm stitch worked from right to left. Bring the needle through from the back of the work at the second pleat from the right. Then work back a stitch over the first two pleats. Move down to the second row, taking the needle through the second and third tubes and work a back stitch over them. Move back up to the first row and work as before with the third and fourth pleats. Continue in the same way across the width of the work. (Diagram 8.)

Honeycomb stitch

This stitch is worked from left to right. Bring the needle up at the top of the first tube and make a back stitch picking up the next tube on the

7

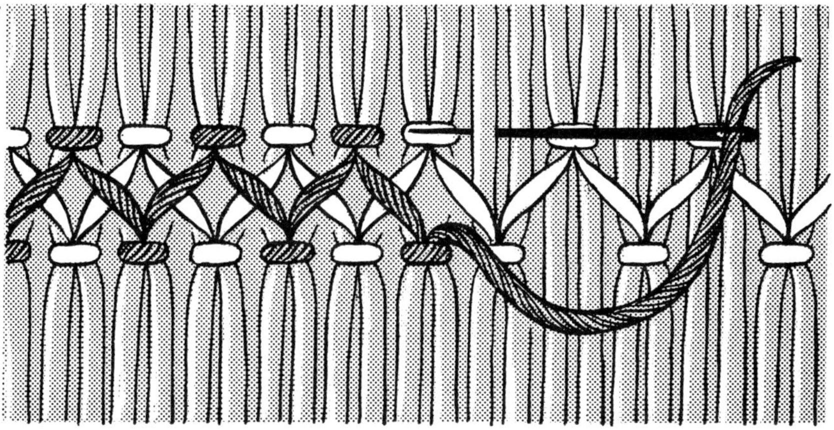

8

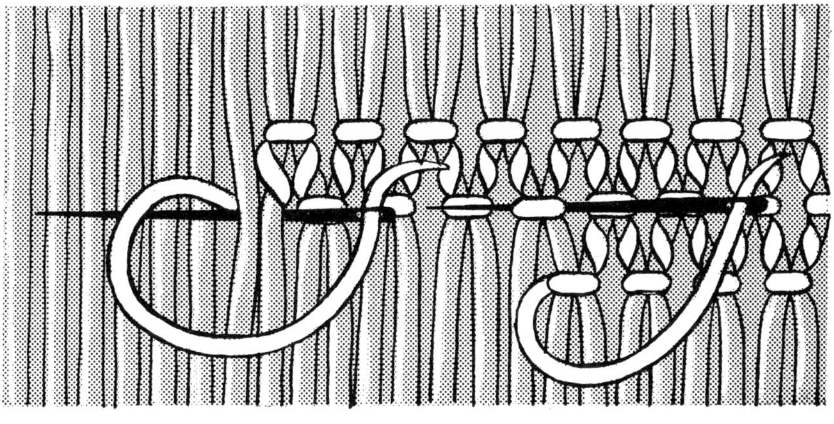

right. Make a second back stitch, slipping the needle down through the pleat and bring it to the right side ready to make the next double back stitch. (Diagram 9.) **Surface honeycomb** stitch is worked in the same way except that the yarn lies on top of the work instead of being taken through to the back. (Diagram 10.)

Double feather stitch

This stitch is worked like ordinary feather stitch, picking up a pleat of the fabric for each stitch and working from right to left. This is a firm-control stitch. (Diagram 11.)

9

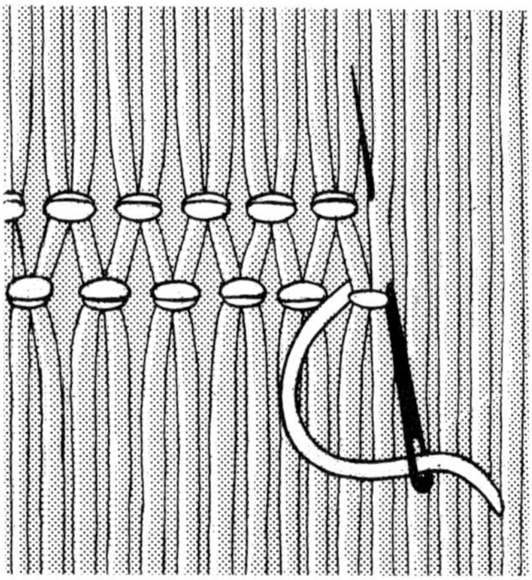

10

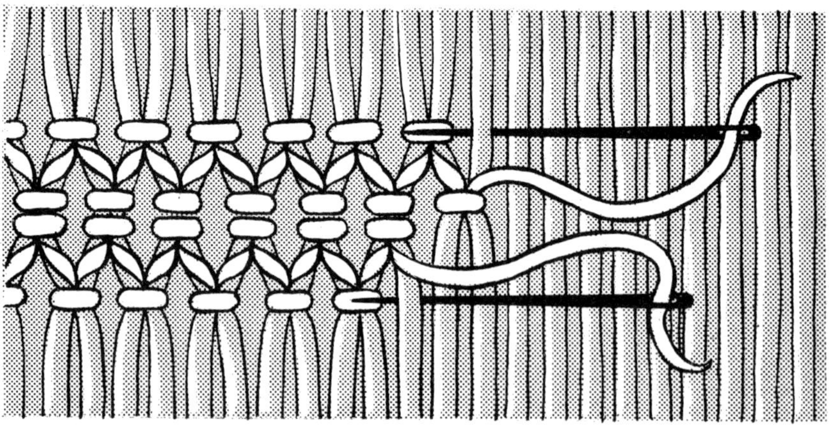

11

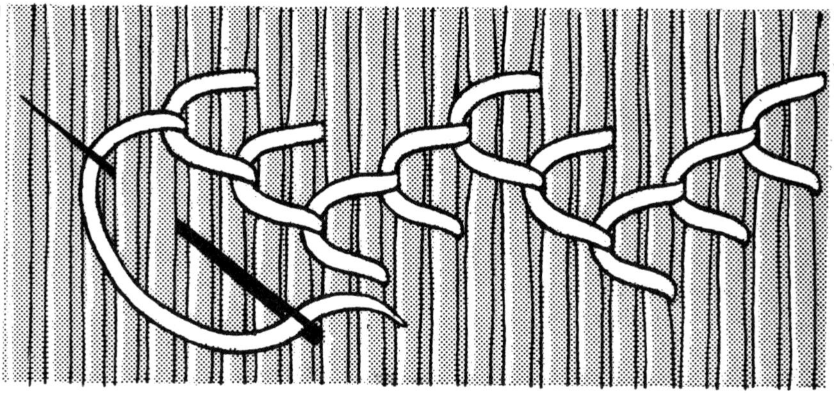

7 MAKING UP & FINISHING

An otherwise beautiful piece of work can be completely ruined by careless workmanship in making up. Although it is far more satisfying to complete a piece of work from start to finish, if you have any doubts about your ability to make up a piece of work, get it done professionally. There are several firms and other organisations which will undertake this service (see *Some useful addresses*, page 115). If you decide to have the work finished professionally, do leave good, deep turnings. In the case of canvas work, it is essential to allow at least 2 in. of unworked canvas for stretching and mounting purposes. A few basic making up techniques are included here for those who prefer to complete their own work.

Mitred corner

A mitre is a fold used to achieve a smooth shaping at a corner and is a technique that is frequently used in many kinds of needlework. To mitre a corner on a hem, fold and press the hem; open out the hem and fold the corner inwards on the inner fold line. Cut off the corner, leaving a small seam allowance of $\frac{1}{8}$ in. to $\frac{1}{4}$ in., depending on the thickness of the fabric. Refold the hem and slip stitch the diagonal line of the mitre and the hem (see diagrams 1, 1a).

1

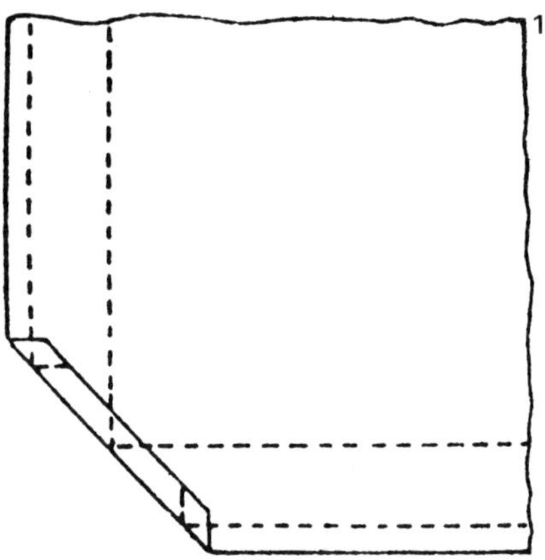

1a

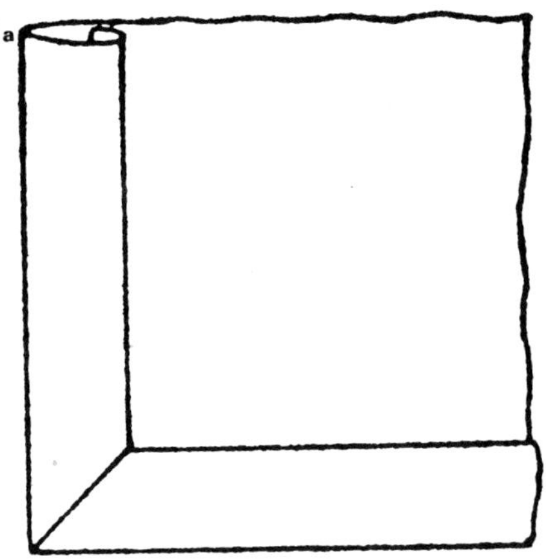

2

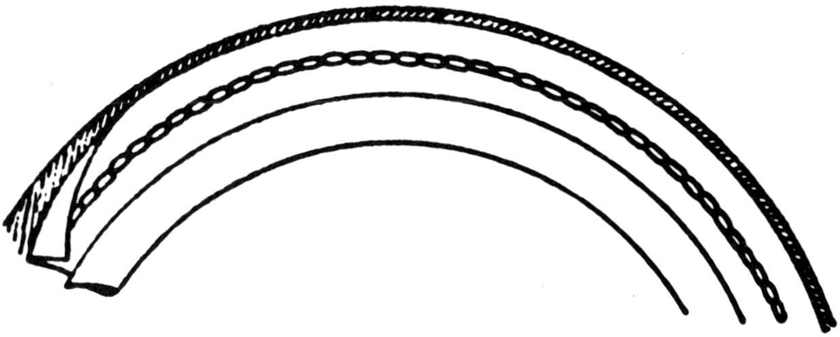

a

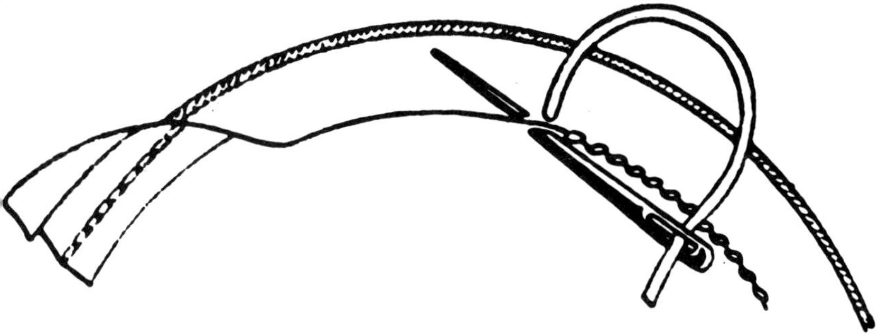

Bias binding hem

A bias binding hem is useful on articles which have a curved or shaped edge where it would be difficult to make an ordinary hem. Lay the bias binding on the fabric edge to edge, with the right sides together. Stitch along the top fold of the binding, stretching the binding slightly on the curve (see diagram). Then turn the binding over to the wrong side of the article and slip stitch along the folded edge of the bias binding (see diagrams 2, 2a).

Making up table and tray cloths

Turn up a hem the desired width all round (following the grain of the fabric on even weave fabrics). Mitre the corners and slip stitch or hem stitch.

Making up a cushion cover

Cut the fabric into equal pieces, then complete the embroidery or decoration on one section. With right sides together, pin and tack the two pieces of fabric. Machine stitch a $\frac{5}{8}$ in. seam, leaving an opening along the centre of one side to allow for the insertion of the zip fastener. If the fabric tends to fray easily, oversew the raw edges. Clip across the corners and turn the cover to the right side. Tack the edges of the opening to the inside and insert the zip fastener following the instructions given on the packet, stitching it in by

3

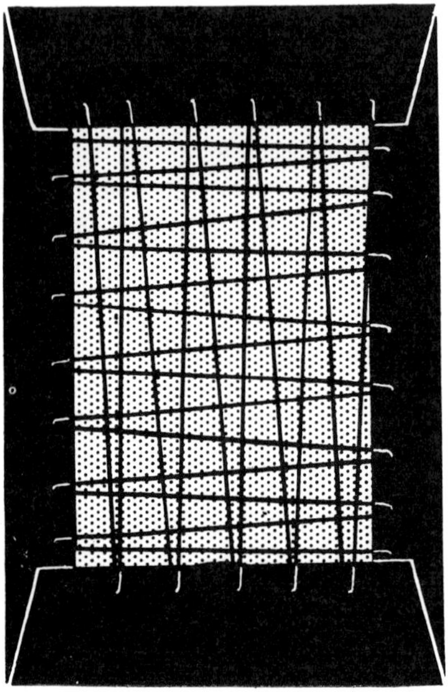

3a

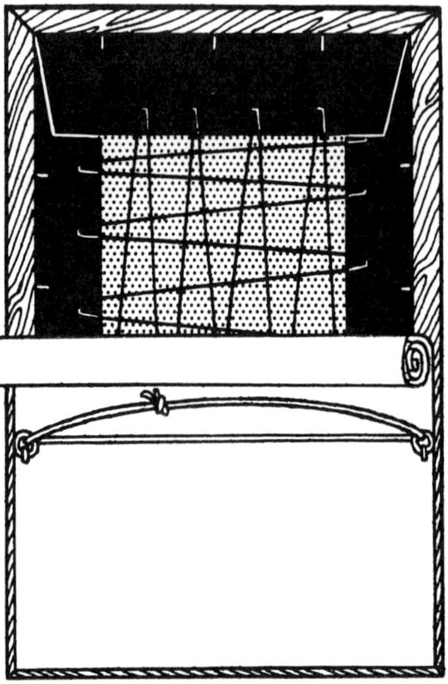

hand. Insert the cushion pad, which should measure 1 in. larger each way than the cover to ensure a plump, well padded cushion.

Canvas work cushions: Trim the excess canvas back to not less than $\frac{5}{8}$ in. from embroidery. Oversew the raw edges of the canvas to prevent fraying. Make up as before, stitching the seams either by machine or back stitch by hand exactly along the edge of the embroidery.

Mounting fabric over hardboard

Embroidered or canvas work panels and pictures can be mounted over hardboard and hung unframed, or the mounted work can be framed under glass. Cut the hardboard to the exact finished size of the picture or panel. Lay the hardboard centrally on the back of the work and lace the fabric or canvas with fine string, picking the fabric up, well in from the raw edge. Lace across the back from side to side and then repeat the process from top to bottom. Pull the lacing up firmly so that the work is stretched evenly without being puckered. Fasten off the ends of the string by knotting them several times (see diagram 3). If the panel is to be hung unframed, neaten the back of the work by sewing a piece of unbleached calico or holland to conceal the lacing (see diagram 3a). If the work is to be framed, it is advisable to take it to a picture framer.

Some useful addresses

The following firms and organisations are suppliers of embroidery, canvas work and needle craft fabrics, yarns and equipment:

The Royal School of Needlework†
25 Prince's Gate
London SW7 1QE

Needlewoman Shop*
146–148 Regent Street
London W1R 6BA

Spinning Jenny
Ivy Terrace
Bradley
Keighley
Yorks BD 209DD

Mace and Nairn
89 Crane Street
Salisbury
Wilts

Canvas work materials and yarns
J B Francis*
4 Glentworth Street
London NW1 5PG

Picture framing
Suttle and Company
71 Great Titchfield Street
London W1P 7FN

All the addresses given above will deal with orders by post. Addresses marked * will mount and make up certain items of work; † indicates that orders will be accepted for making slate frames to size.

Yarn spinners

J & P Coats (UK) Ltd
PO Box 31
Central Office
12 Seedhill Road
Paisley PA1 1JT

H G Twilley
Roman Hill
Little Casterton Road
Stamford
Lincs PE9 1BG

Lister Wools Ltd
PO Box 37
Providence Mills
Westgate
Wakefield
Yorks WF2 9SF

Queries concerning the yarns specified in this book should be referred to the appropriate firm.

8 STITCHES

Embroidery stitches

Instructions are given here for the stitches mentioned throughout the preceding chapters, with the exception of rug and smocking stitches which are given in the appropriate chapters.

Straight stitch

These are single spaced stitches worked either in a regular or irregular arrangement. The stitches can be of varying sizes but they should not be too long or too loose. (Diagram 1.)

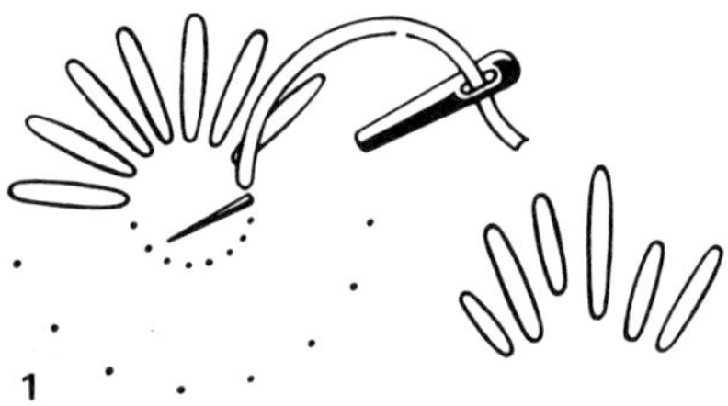

1

Satin stitch

Straight stitches are worked closely across the shape as shown in the diagram. If desired, running or chain stitches may be used to form a padding underneath the stitch to give a raised effect. Avoid working the stitches too long or they may pull out of position. (Diagram 2.)

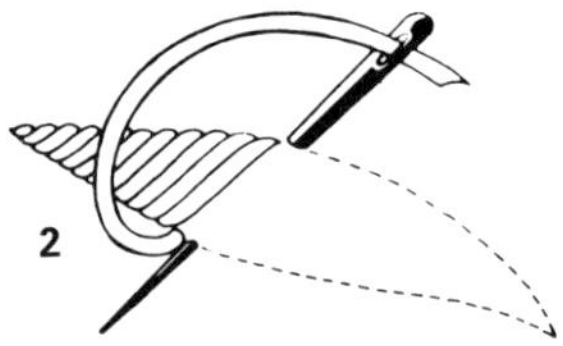

2

Long and short stitch

This form of satin stitch is so named as the stitches are of varying lengths. It is often used to fill a shape which is too large or too irregular to be covered by satin stitch. It is also used to achieve a shaded effect. (Diagram 3.)

3

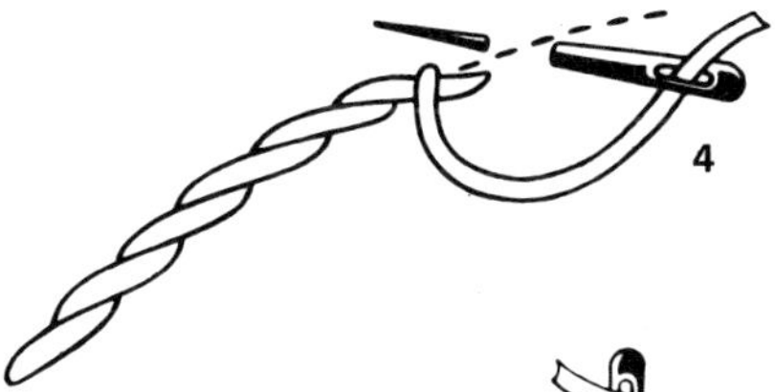

Stem stitch
Work from left to right taking regular, slightly slanting stitches along the line of the design. The thread always emerges on the left hand side of the previous stitch. (Diagram 4.)

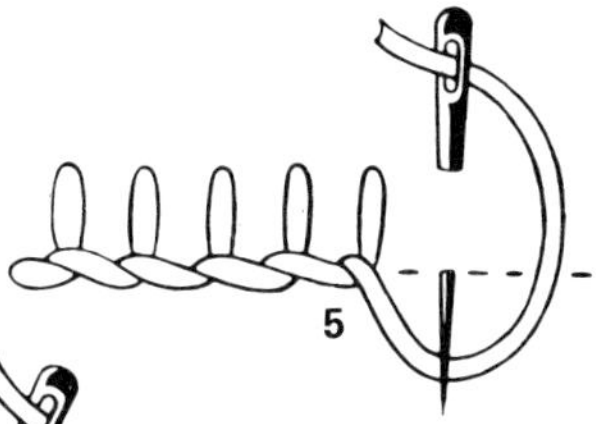

Buttonhole stitch

Bring the thread out on the lower line, insert the needle in position in the upper line, taking a straight downward stitch with the thread under the needle point. Pull up the stitch to form a loop and repeat. (Diagram 5.)

Chain stitch
Bring the thread out at the top of the line and hold it down with the left thumb. Insert the needle where it last emerged and bring the point out a short distance away. Pull the thread through, keeping the working thread under the needle point. (Diagram 6.)

French knots
Bring the needle out at the required position, hold the thread down with the left thumb and encircle the thread twice with the needle as at A. Still holding the thread firmly, twist the needle back to the starting point and insert it close to where the first emerged (see arrow). Pull the thread through to the back and secure for a single French knot or pass onto the position of the next stitch as at B. (Diagram 7.)

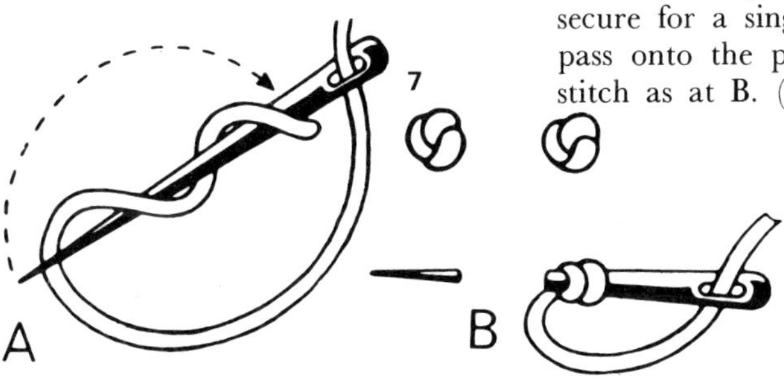

Counted thread and canvas work

Although grouped under this heading, some of the following stitches are suitable for more general use.

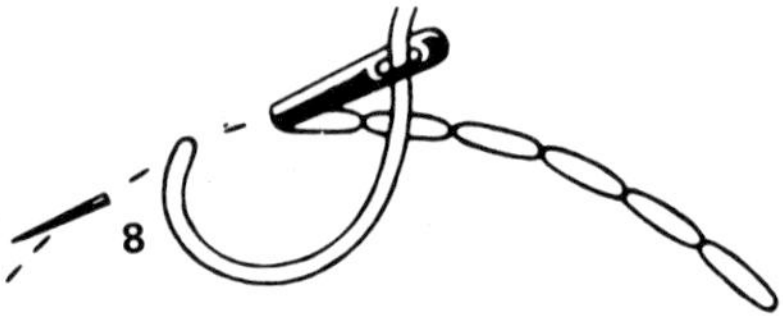

8

Back stitch

This stitch must be worked small and regular. It can be interlaced or whipped with a self or contrasting coloured yarn. (Diagrams 8, 9.)

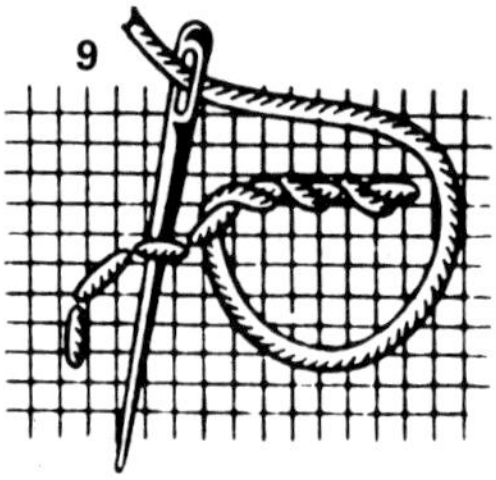

9

Satin stitch

This is worked like ordinary satin stitch but over the counted threads of the fabric. (Diagram 10.)

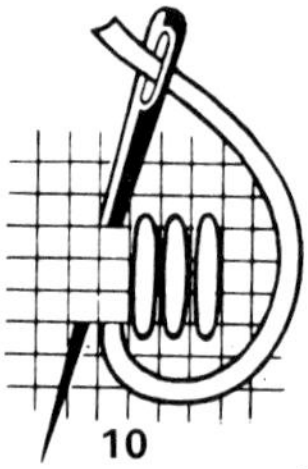

10

Cross stitch

This stitch can be worked over any number of threads on an even weave fabric. The same number of threads must be worked over both vertically and horizontally. (Diagram 11.)

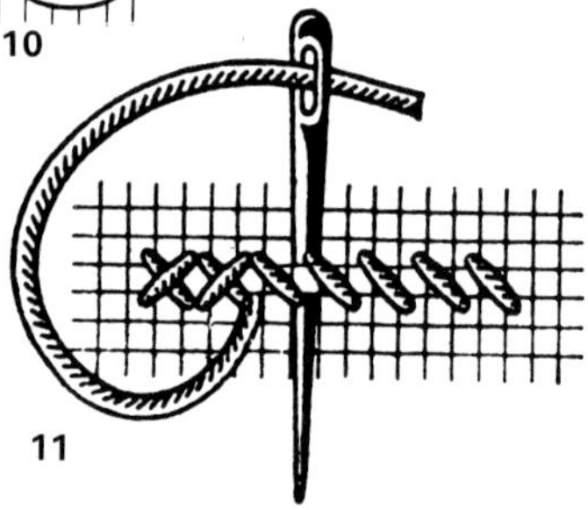

11

Sheaf stitch

An attractive filling stitch consisting of three vertical satin stitches tied across the centre with two horizontal overcasting stitches. The overcasting stitches are worked round the satin stitches; the needle only entering the fabric to pass to the next sheaf. (Diagram 12.)

12 1 2

Fern stitch

This stitch consists of three straight stitches of equal length radiating from a central point. (Diagram 13.)

Star stitch or eyelet

The eyelet consists of eight stitches worked over a square of fabric, eight threads each way, all the stitches being worked from the same central hole. (Diagram 14, opposite.)

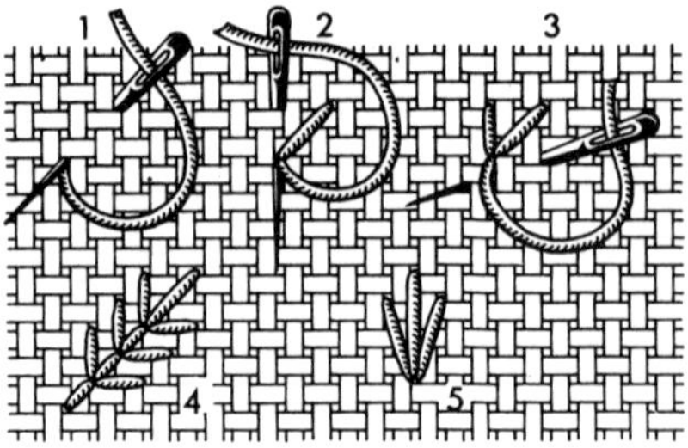

13

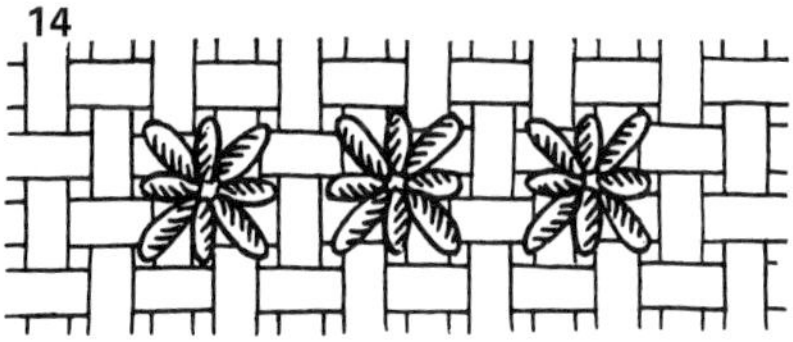

14

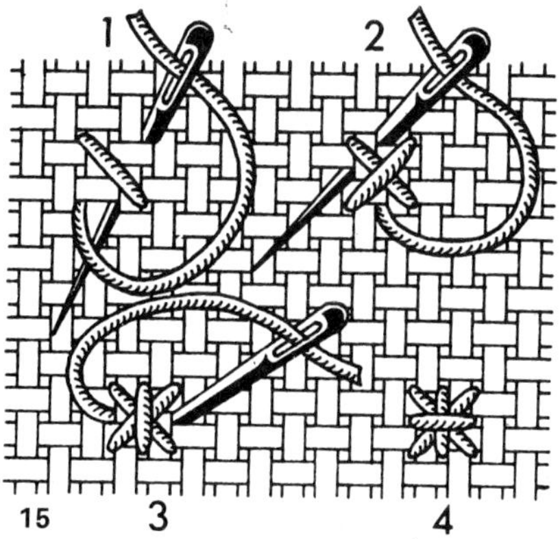

15

Double cross stitch

Work a single cross stitch, then work a second cross stitch over this as shown. (Diagram 15.)

Double faggot filling

This stitch is worked in diagonal rows of back stitch, each stitch being worked over two threads of fabric twice. (Diagrams 16, 17.)

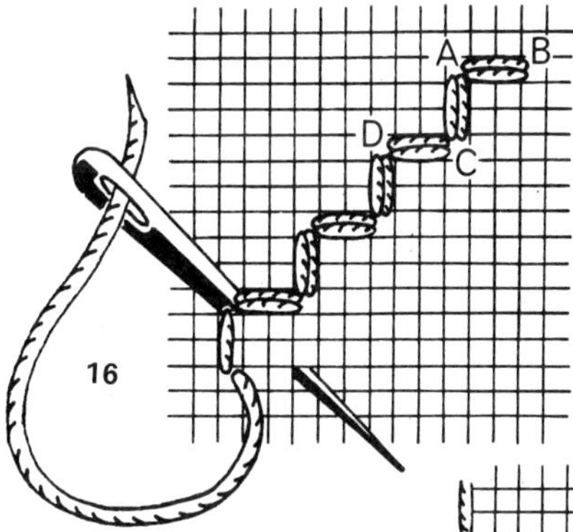

16

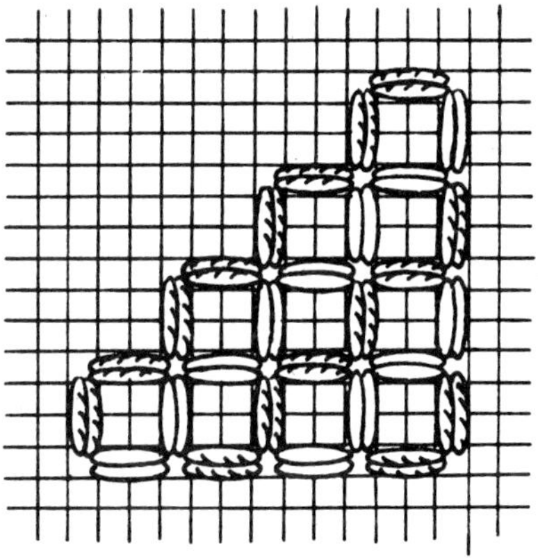

17

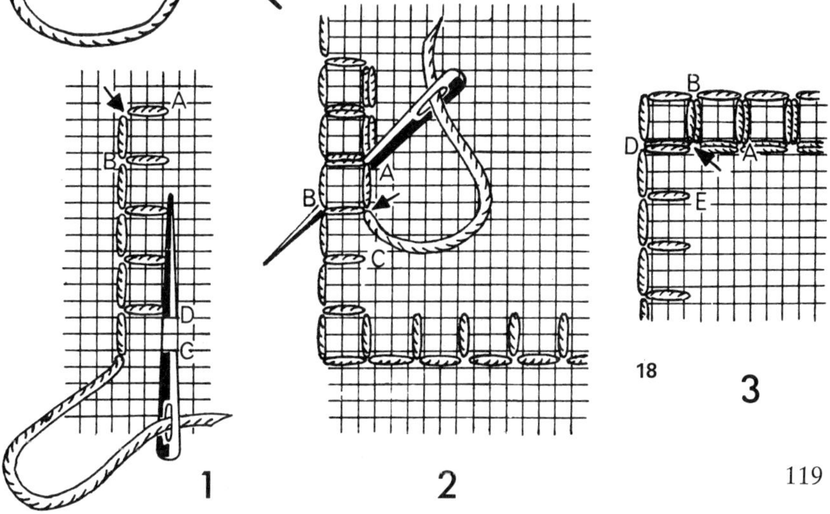

18

Four-sided stitch
This stitch is worked from right to left and can be used as a border or a filling.

1 Bring the thread through at the arrow; insert the needle at A, bring it through at B.

2 Insert the needle at the arrow, bring it out at C.

3 Insert the needle again at A and bring it out at B. Continue in this way to the end of the row or close the end for a single four-sided stitch.

For a filling stitch: 4 Turn the fabric round for next and following rows and work in the same way. Pull all the stitches firmly. (Diagram 18 on previous page.)

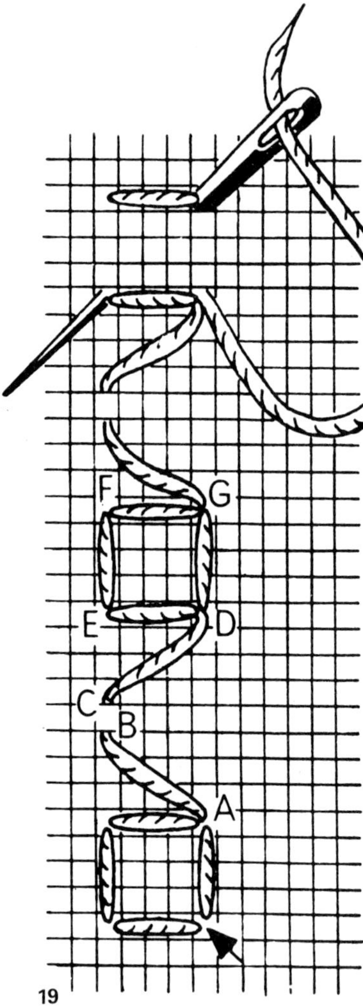

19

Linked four-sided stitch
This is worked over an even number of threads each way as shown. The linking stitch is taken from the top of the four-sided stitch across three threads and down four, picking up two threads, and the needle is then taken up four and across three threads to commence the next four-sided stitch. (Diagram 19.)

Coil filling stitch
This stitch is worked over the counted thread of the fabric as shown and the yarn pulled firmly to give an open, lace like filling. (Diagrams 20, 21.)

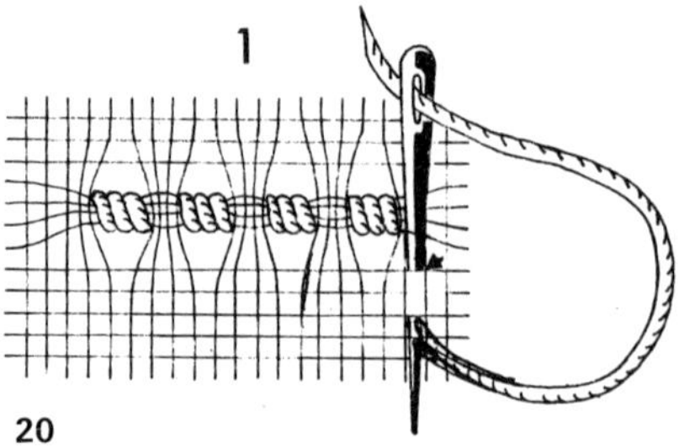

20

Hem stitch
Measure the required depth of hem, plus the turnings and withdraw required number of threads (usually one to three threads). Do not withdraw the threads right across the fabric, but only to form a square or rectangle. Cut the threads at the centre and withdraw gradually out-

wards on each side to within the hem measurement, leaving a sufficient length of thread at the corners in order to darn the ends invisibly. Turn back the hem to the space of the drawn threads, mitre the corners and tack.

Bring the working thread out two threads down from the space of the drawn threads through the folded hem at the right hand side, pass the needle behind four loose threads, bringing the needle out two threads down through all the folds of the hem in readiness to work the next stitch. (Diagram 22.)

Wheat-ear stitch
This stitch is worked from the top downwards and the needle does not go through the fabric when the chain loop is made. (Diagram 23.)

Tent stitch
Tent stitch can be worked horizontally or vertically, but over a large area it is best to work diagonally to avoid pulling the canvas out of shape. (Diagrams 24, 25.)

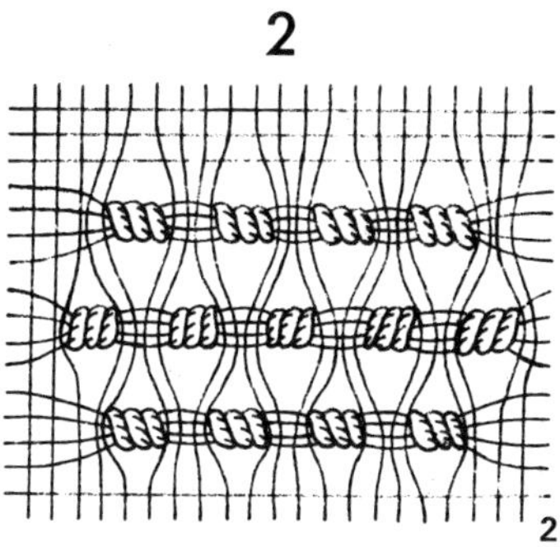

21

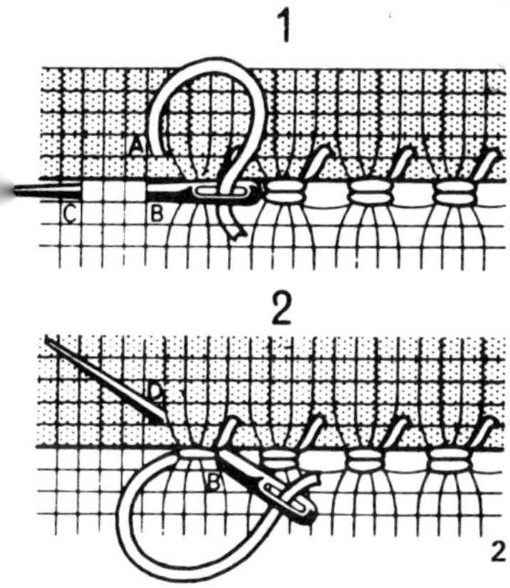

22

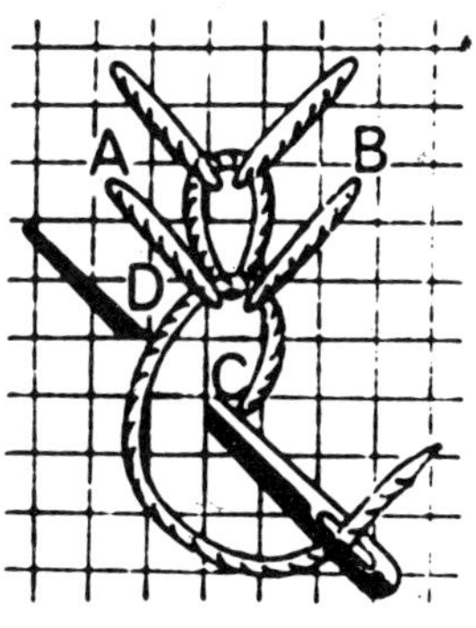

23

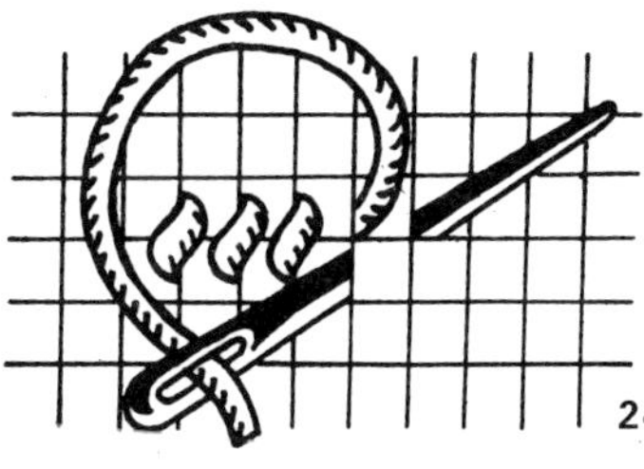
24

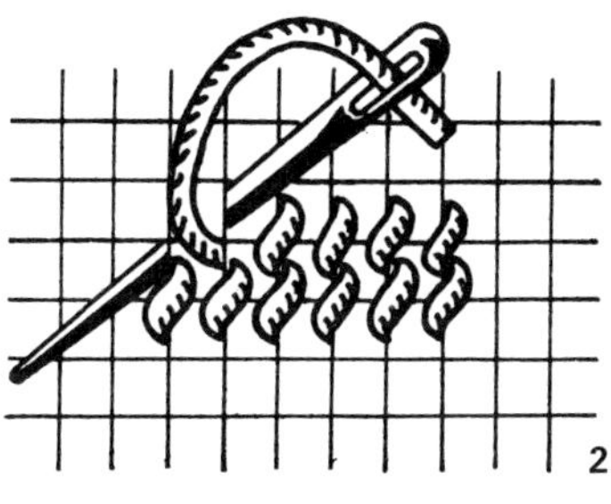
25

9 CROCHET

by Coralyn Walton

If you don't know how to crochet, it is a technique that is very well worth learning because it is simple to do and extremely versatile in its uses. If you have plenty of patience you will enjoy working in spidery cotton thread and equally, if you are the sort of person who likes to see results quickly, you can achieve these working in wool. It is easy to learn because, basically, crochet has only one stitch, that of pulling a thread through a loop to form the next loop. The variations on this are endless and the results can be a fine lace cobweb or a firm, textured fabric.

Tracing its origins at least as far back as the ancient Egyptians crochet has become high fashion in the last decade and shows no signs of losing its regained popularity.

Equipment

Crochet hooks come in varying sizes from the very fine steel ones for working with fine cotton, to the larger alloy hooks which are used with wool. As well as the type of yarn, the required tension decides the size of the hook and it is always vital to obtain the correct tension before starting any project. Should the suggested size not give the correct tension, adjust the hook size until the tension measurements are right. If the work is tight and there are too many stitches and rows to the inch, adjust to a larger hook until the correct one is found. Conversely, if the work is loose, choose a smaller size of hook. When making up work, stainless steel dressmaking pins, a tape measure and a blunt-ended wool needle will be required.

If you are starting from scratch, turn to Chapter 10 where you will find instructions for the beginner together with details and diagrams of how to do the stitches used in the following designs.

Abbreviations

alt	alternate	dc	double crochet	in.	inch(es)
beg	beginning	dec	decrease	inc	increase
blk(s)	block(s)	dtr	double treble	No	number
ch	chain	gr(s)	group(s)	p	picot
cl	cluster	htr	half treble	patt	pattern

qd tr	quadruple treble	sp(s)	space(s)	tr	treble
rem	remaining	ss	slip stitch	tr tr	triple treble
rep	repeat	st(s)	stitch(es)	WS	wrong side
RS	right side	tog	together	yrh	yarn round hook

Lace curtain, with detail inset (see overleaf and page 125)

Lace curtain (See previous page)

This beautiful, lacy curtain silhouettes against the window in an intricate filigree. The instructions are for a small curtain measuring 36 in. by 24 in., but the pattern could be used to make a larger one or, if you prefer, a bed-spread. You will need:

Coats Mercer Crochet Cotton No 20: quantity according to required size (1 ball makes 3 motifs).

A No 1·00 crochet hook.

Tension

Each motif measures 6 in. square worked on No 1·00 hook.

Motif

Using No 1·00 hook, make 10ch. Join with ss to form ring.

1st round: 4ch to count as first dtr, leaving last loop of each on hook make 2dtr into ring, yrh and draw through all loops on hook, 3ch, *leaving last loop of each on hook make 3dtr into ring, yrh and draw through all 4 loops (called 1cl), 3ch, rep from * 6 times more, ss to 4th of 4ch. 8 petals.

2nd round: Ss along to first sp, 4ch to count as first dtr, 3dtr in same sp, 3ch, *4dtr into next sp, 3ch, rep from * 6 times more, ss to 4th of 4ch.

3rd round: 4ch to count as first dtr, 1dtr in same st, 2dtr into each of next 3dtr, 3ch, 1dtr into next dtr, 2dtr into each of next 2dtr, 1dtr into next dtr, 3ch, *2dtr into each of next 4dtr, 3ch, 1dtr into next dtr, 2dtr into each of next 2dtr, 1dtr into next dtr, 3ch, rep from * twice more, ss to 4th of 4ch.

4th round: 1ch, *miss first dtr of group of 8dtr, 1dc into each of next 6dtr, miss next dtr, (5ch, 1dtr into each of next 3dtr) twice, 5ch, rep from * 3 times more.

5th round: *Miss first dc, 1dc into each of next 5dc, 5ch, 1dtr into each of next 3dtr, 5ch, 1dc into next sp, 5ch, 1dtr into each of next 3dtr, 5ch, rep from * 3 times more.

6th round: *Miss first dc, 1dc into each of next 4dc, 5ch, 1dtr into each of next 3dtr, 5ch, (1dc into next sp, 5ch) twice, 1dtr into each of next 3dtr, 5ch, rep from * 3 times more.

7th round: *Miss first dc, 1dc into each of next 3dc, 5ch, 1dtr into each of next 3dtr, 5ch, 1dc in next sp, 5ch, 4dtr into next sp, 5ch, 1dc into next sp, 5ch, 1dtr into each of next 3dtr, 5ch, rep from * 3 times more.

8th round: *Miss first dc, 1dc into each of next 2dc, 5ch, 1dtr into each of next 3dtr, 5ch, 1dc into next sp, 5ch, 4dtr into next sp, 7ch, 4dtr into next sp, 5ch, 1dc into next sp, 5ch, 1dtr into each of next 3dtr, 5ch, rep from * 3 times more, join with ss to first dc.

9th round: Ss along first 5ch to first dtr, 4ch to count as first dtr, 1dtr into each of next 2dtr, *(5ch, 1dc into next sp) twice, 5ch, into 7ch sp make (1cl, 5ch) 4 times, (1dc into next sp, 5ch) twice, 1dtr into each of next 3dtr, 1dtr into each of next 3dtr, rep from * 3 times more but omitting last 3dtr and ending with ss into 4th of 4ch.

10th round: 4ch, into sp between first 2grs of 3dtr work 2dtr leaving the last loop of each on hook, yrh and draw through all loops, *5ch, 1dc into next sp, 5ch, 1cl into next sp, 5ch, 1dc into next sp, (5ch, 1cl into next sp) 3 times, 5ch, 1dc into next sp, 5ch, 1cl into next sp, 5ch, 1dc into next sp, 5ch, 1cl between 2grs of 3dtr, rep from * 3 times more but omitting last cl and ending with ss in top of first cl. Fasten off.

To make up

Make 24 motifs altogether, or the required number. Pin out each motif, cover with a damp cloth and leave until cloth is completely dry. Remove pins. Join the motifs in rows as required, using small overcast stitches between the 5 cluster along each side and leaving the corner clusters free. Starch lightly and mount on a thin brass rod.

Petal bedspread (See overleaf and pages 127–134)

This fine bedspread is destined to become a family heirloom. The distinctive centre section is worked in a series of large and small motifs; the border is worked separately. The bedspread measures 65 in. by 76 in., excluding the border. You will need:

Coats Mercer Crochet No 30: 86 balls.
A No 1·75 crochet hook.

To make the centre motifs, work as follows:

1st petal

Using No 1·25 hook, make 19ch.

1st row: (WS) Into 5th ch from hook work 1dc, *1dc into next ch, rep from * to end. Turn. 15dc.

2nd row: 1ch, working into the back loop only of each st (called in relief), 1dc into each of 15dc, turn. *NB* Each row is begun at first dc as well as having a turning ch.

3rd row: 1ch, 1dc in relief into each of next 15dc, into 1ch at beg of 2nd row work 1dc, 1ch and 1dc, on the opposite side of foundation ch work 1dc into each of the 15ch, turn.

4th row: 1ch, 1dc in relief into each of next 16dc, into 1ch sp work 1dc, 1ch and 1dc, on the opposite side of petal work 1dc in relief into each of 15dc, turn.

5th row: 3ch to form 1p, 1dc in relief into each of next 16dc, into 1ch sp work 1dc, 1ch and 1dc, on opposite side of petal work 1dc in relief into each of 15dc, turn.

6th row: 3ch to form 1p, 1dc in relief into each st, omitting centre 1ch and omitting last st of row, turn.

7th row: 1ch, 1dc in relief into each of next 16dc, into next st work 1dc, 1ch and 1dc, 1dc in relief into each of next 16 sts, turn.

8th row: 1ch, 1dc in relief into each st of row omitting last st, turn.

9th row: 1ch, 1dc in relief into each of next 16dc, into next st work 1dc, 1ch and 1dc, 1dc in relief into each of next 16dc, turn.

10th row: 3ch to form 1p, 1dc in relief into each st to within last 2 sts, into next st work 1dc, 3ch to form 1p and 1dc. Fasten off.

Petal bedspread, with detail inset (see pages 125–134)

2nd petal
Work as for first petal to 9th row.

10th row: 3ch, 1dc in relief into each of 11dc, place first petal behind 2nd petal, wrong sides tog, and work 1dc in relief inserting hook into next st of 2nd petal and 12th st of first petal at the same time, work 1dc in relief into each of next 3 sts of both petals, then complete second petal as first.

The 3rd petal of each motif is worked as for the 2nd; the 4th petal is worked joining it to both the 3rd and first petals in the same way.

Border motif
Join with ss to left-hand p of any petal, 4ch, 1tr into same p, *into right-hand p of next petal work 2tr tr, 8ch, into p at right-hand end of 6th row work 2tr, 5ch and 2tr, 7ch, 1dc into p on 5th row (centre point of petal), 7ch, into p at left-hand end of 6th row work 2tr, 5ch and 2tr, 8ch, 2tr tr into left-hand p of same petal, rep from * 3 times more but omitting last 2tr tr, join with ss to first tr tr, ss to 2nd tr tr.

2nd round: *1dc between 2grs of 2tr tr, 9ch, into next 5ch sp work 2tr, 6ch and 2tr, 8ch, 1dc into next dc, 8ch, into next 5ch sp work 2tr, 6ch and 2tr, 9ch, rep from * to end, join with ss to first dc.

3rd round: 5ch, 1dc into 4th ch from hook, *7ch, into the 6ch sp work (2tr, 4ch, 1dc into first of these 4ch) 6 times, 2tr into same 6ch sp, 7ch, then 4ch and 1dc into first of these 4ch, 1dc into next dc, 4ch, 1dc into first of these 4ch, rep from * all round but omitting last dc and p on last rep, join with ss to 1ch at beg of round. Fasten off.

Joining large motifs
Join 2nd motif to first in the 3rd round as follows:

In the 6ch sp of the 2nd motif work (2tr, 1p) 3 times, then 2tr, 2ch, drop loop from hook, insert hook in 4th p on the side of first motif (counting right to left), and insert hook into dropped loop, draw loop through, 2ch, in same sp of 2nd motif work 2tr, join as previously to 5th p of first motif, 2tr in same sp of 2nd motif, then 1p and 2tr, 7ch, 1p, 1dc, 1p, 7ch, into the next 6ch sp work 2tr, 1p and 2tr, join to the 2p corresponding on the side of the first motif, in the same sp of the 2nd motif work (2tr, 1p) 3 times, then 2tr, continue to end as for first motif.

Work 3rd motif in same way, joining to the 2nd motif. Continue until 16 motifs have been joined.

Work another row of 16 motifs, joining each motif to the corresponding motif of the first row and to the previous motif on the same row. Continue until there are 14 rows each of 16 motifs.

Small connecting motifs
Where 4 large motifs have been joined to form a rectangle, one small motif fills the centre hole.

Using No 1·25 hook, make 20ch. Join with ss to first ch to form a ring. Work 20ch, join with ss to previous ss to form a second ring. Place the rings one over the other.

1st round: 4ch, *into the double thickness ring work 7ch, 3ch, rep from * twice more, 7dc into ring, ss into first of 4ch.

2nd round: Ss into first 3ch sp, 3ch, into same 3ch sp and keeping the last loop of each on the hook work 2tr, yrh and pull through all 3 loops, 5ch, keeping last loop of each on hook work 3tr, yrh and pull through all 4 loops (called 1cl), *6ch, into next 3ch sp work 1cl, 5ch and 1cl, rep from * twice more, 6ch, ss into top of first cl.

3rd round: Ss into first 5ch sp, 3ch, into same sp and keeping the last loop of each on the hook work 2tr, yrh and pull through all 3 loops, *1ch, drop loop from hook, insert hook into the 2nd of 3p free on side of large motif, insert hook into dropped loop and draw loop through, 2ch, join in same way to the 3rd p, 3ch, join to first free p on next large motif, 2ch, join to 2nd p, 1ch, 1cl into same 5ch sp, (4ch, ss into first of these 4ch) 6 times, 1cl into next 5ch sp, rep from * 3 times more, ss into first cl. Fasten off.

Half motif

Using No 1·25 hook, make 11ch, into 2nd ch from hook work 1ss, 10ch, ss into the first ch worked.

1st row: 2ch, 1dc into first ch of ring, into ring work 7dc, 3ch and 7dc, 3ch, ss into 1ch sp, turn.

2nd row: Ss into 3ch sp, 3ch, into same 3ch sp work 2tr keeping last loop of each on hook, yrh and pull through all loops on hook, 6ch, into 3ch sp work 1cl, 5ch and 1cl, 6ch, into next ch sp work 1cl.

3rd row: 3ch, join in the usual way to 3rd and 2nd last p of lower left-hand corner of large motif to the right, 1ch, 1dc in top of previous cl, (4ch, ss into first of these 4ch) 6 times, make next join in usual way followed by a row of 6p, 1cl in top of left-hand cl, join to p of left-hand motif.

Border

Using No 1·25 hook make 163ch.

1st row: Into 4th ch from hook make 1tr, 2ch, miss 4ch, into next st work 4tr, 3ch and 4tr (called 1gr), 8ch, miss 9ch, 1gr into next ch, (2ch, miss 2ch, 1tr in next ch) 3 times, 2ch, miss 2ch, 5tr, (5ch, miss 3ch, 6dc) 6 times, 5ch, miss 3ch, 16tr, 5ch, miss 5ch, 1tr, 5ch, miss 5ch, 4tr, 2ch, miss 2ch, 4tr, 5ch, miss 5ch, 1tr, 5ch, miss 5ch, 16tr, 2ch, miss 2ch, 4tr.

12ch, into 10th ch from hook work 1tr, into 11th ch work 1tr, into 12th ch work 1tr (to inc), 1tr in first tr of first row, 2ch, miss 2tr, 1tr in next st, 2tr into 2ch sp, 1tr in next tr, 8ch, miss 6tr, 1tr in next tr, 8ch,

1tr in last of 16tr of previous row, 7tr in next ch sp, 7tr in next ch sp, 1tr in next tr, 5ch, 2tr in next 2ch sp, 5ch, 1tr in last of next 4tr, 7tr in next ch sp, 7tr in next ch sp, 1tr in next tr, 8ch, miss 6tr, 1tr in next tr, 8ch, 1tr in last of 16tr of previous row, 3tr in next ch sp, (5ch, 1tr in 3rd dc, 1tr in 4th dc, 5ch, 2tr in next ch sp) 6 times, 5ch, miss 2tr, 3tr, 2tr in next 2ch sp, 1 tr in next tr, (2ch, 1tr in next tr) twice, 2ch, into 3ch sp of gr work 1gr, 8ch, 1gr into 3ch sp of next gr, 2ch, 1tr into next tr, 1tr into 3rd of 3ch at beg of first row.

3rd row 3ch, miss first tr, 1tr into next tr, 2ch, 1gr into next gr, 5ch, 1dc into ch from both first and 2nd rows, 5ch, 1gr into next gr, 2ch, 1tr into next tr, 2ch, 1tr into next tr, 2tr into 2ch sp, 4tr, 5ch, (2dc into next ch sp, 1dc into each of next 2tr, 2dc into next ch sp, 5ch, miss 2tr) 6 times, 3tr into next ch sp, 1tr into each of next 4 sts, 8ch, 1dc into next tr, 8ch, 13tr, 5ch, 2dc into next ch sp, 1dc into each of next 2tr, 2dc into next ch sp, 5ch, miss 3tr, 13tr, 8ch, 1dc into next tr, 8ch, 4tr, 2tr into next 2ch sp, 1tr into next tr, 2ch, miss 2 sts, 1tr into next tr, 3tr into last ch sp of row.

4th row: 12ch, 1tr into 10th ch from hook, 1tr into each of 11th and 12th ch from hook, 1tr into first tr, 2ch, miss 2tr, 1tr into next tr, 2tr into next 2ch sp, 7tr, 8ch, 1dc into next dc, 8ch, 11tr, 5ch, 2tr into next ch sp, 5ch, 1tr into 3rd dc, 1tr into 4th dc, 5ch, 2tr into next ch sp, 5ch, miss 2tr, 11tr, 8ch, 1dc into next dc, 8ch, 7tr, 3tr into next ch sp, (5ch, 1tr into 3rd dc, 1tr into 4th dc, 5ch, 2tr into next ch sp) 5 times, 5ch, 1tr into 3rd dc, 1tr into 4th dc, 5ch, 2tr into next ch sp, 4tr, 2ch, miss 2tr, 1tr, 2ch, 1tr into next tr, 2ch, 1gr into next gr, 8ch, 1gr into next gr, 2ch, 1tr into next tr, 1tr into 3rd ch at end.

5th row: 3ch, 1tr into 2nd tr, 2ch, 1gr into next gr, 8ch, 1gr into next gr, 2ch, 1tr into next tr, 2ch, 1tr into next tr, 2ch, 1tr into next tr, 2ch, miss 2tr, 3tr, 2tr into next ch sp, 5ch, (6dc, 5ch, miss 2tr) 5 times, 3tr into next ch sp, 10tr, *5ch, 1dc into all ch from previous 3 rows, 5ch, 1tr into next dc, 5ch, 1dc into all ch from previous 3 rows, 5ch*, 7tr, 5ch, 6dc, 5ch, miss next 2tr, 6dc, 5ch, miss 4tr, 7tr, rep from * to * once more, 10tr, 2tr into next 2ch sp, 1tr into next tr, 2ch, miss 2tr, 1tr into next tr, 3tr into last ch sp.

6th row: 12ch, work 1tr into each of the 10th, 11th and 12th ch from hook, 1tr into next tr, 2ch, miss 2tr, 1tr into next tr, 2tr into next 2ch sp, 13tr, 5ch, 1tr into next tr, 5ch, 5tr, (5ch, 2tr into next ch sp, 5ch, 1tr into 3rd dc, 1 tr into 4th dc) twice, 5ch, 2tr into next ch sp, 5ch, miss 3tr, 4tr, 5ch, 1tr into next tr, 5ch, 13tr, 3tr into next ch sp, (5ch, 1tr into 3rd dc, 1tr into 4th dc, 5ch, 2tr into next ch sp) 5 times, 5ch, miss 2tr, 3tr, 2tr into next 2ch sp, 1tr into next tr, 2ch, 1tr into next tr, 2ch, 1tr into next tr, 2ch, 1gr into next gr, 5ch, 1dc into ch of both previous 2 rows, 5ch, 1gr into next gr, 2ch, 2tr.

7th row: 3ch, 1tr into 2nd tr, 2ch, 1gr into next gr, 8ch, 1gr into next gr, 2ch, 1tr into next tr, 2ch, 1tr into next tr, 2tr into next ch sp, 4tr, 5ch, (6dc, 5ch, miss next 2tr) 5 times, 3tr into next ch sp, 1tr into next tr, 8ch, miss 6 sts,

1tr, 8ch, miss 7 sts, 1tr into next tr, 7tr into next ch sp, 7tr into next ch sp, 1tr into next tr, 5ch, (6dc, 5ch, miss 2tr) twice, 6dc, 5ch, miss 3tr, 1tr into next st, 7tr into next ch sp, 7tr into next ch sp, 1tr into next tr, 8ch, miss 6 sts, 1tr, 8ch, miss 7 sts, 1tr, 2tr into next 2ch sp, 1tr into next tr, 2ch, miss 2 sts, 1tr into next tr, 3tr into last ch sp.

8th row: 12ch, work 1tr into each of the 10th, 11th and 12th ch from hook, 1tr into first tr of row, 2ch, miss 2tr, 1tr into next tr, 2tr into next 2ch sp, 4tr, 8ch, 1dc into next tr, 8ch, 13tr, (5ch, 2tr into next ch sp, 5ch, 1tr into 3rd dc, 1tr into 4th dc) 3 times, 5ch, 2tr into next ch sp, 5ch, miss 2tr, 14tr, 8ch, 1dc into next tr, 8ch, 4tr, 3tr into next ch sp, (5ch, 1tr into 3rd dc, 1tr into 4th dc, 5ch, 2tr into next ch sp) 4 times, 5ch, 1tr into 3rd dc, 1tr into 4th dc, 5ch, 2tr into next ch sp, 4tr, 2ch, miss 2tr, 1tr, 2ch, 1tr into next tr, 2ch, 1gr into next gr, 8ch, 1gr into next gr, 2ch, 2tr.

9th row: 3ch, 1tr into 2nd tr, 2ch, 1gr into next gr, 5ch, 1dc into both ch of 2 previous rows, 5ch, 1gr into next gr, 2ch, 1tr into next tr, 2ch, 1tr into next tr, 2ch, 1tr into next tr, 2ch, miss 2tr, 5tr, (5ch, miss 2tr, 6dc) 4 times, 5ch, 3tr into next ch sp, 7tr, 8ch, 1dc into next dc, 8ch, 11tr, 5ch, (6dc, 5ch, miss 2tr) 3 times, 6dc, 5ch, miss 2tr, 11tr, 8ch, 1dc into next dc, 8ch, 1tr into each of next 7tr, 2tr into next 2ch sp, 1tr into next tr, 2ch, miss 2tr, 1tr, 3tr into last ch sp.

10th row: 12ch, 1tr into each of the 10th, 11th and 12th ch from hook, 1tr into first tr, 2ch, miss 2tr, 1tr into next tr, 12tr (ie the first 2 of these worked into the next 2ch sp), *5ch, 1dc into all ch from 3 previous rows, 5ch, 1tr into next tr, 5ch, 1dc into all ch from 3 previous rows, 5ch*, 7tr, (5ch, 2tr into next ch sp, 5ch, 1dc into 3rd dc, 1dc into 4th dc) 4 times, 5ch, 2tr into next ch sp, 5ch, miss 3tr, 8tr, rep from * to * once more, 12tr (ie the last 2 of these worked into the ch sp), (5ch, 1tr into 3rd dc, 1tr into 4th dc, 5ch, 2tr into next ch sp) 4 times, 5ch, miss 2tr, 6tr, 2ch, 1tr into next tr, 2ch, 1tr into next tr, 2ch, 1gr into next gr, 8ch, 1gr into next gr, 2ch, 2tr.

11th row: 3ch, 1tr into 2nd tr, 2ch, 1gr into next gr, 8ch, 1gr into next gr, 2ch, 1tr into next tr, 2ch, 7tr, 5ch, (6dc, 5ch, miss 2tr) 4 times, 2tr into next ch sp, 12tr, 5ch, 1tr into next tr, 5ch, 4tr, 5ch, (6dc, 5ch, miss 2tr) 4 times, 6dc, 5ch, miss 3tr, 4tr, 5ch, 1tr into next tr, 5ch, 16tr, 2ch, miss 2tr, 1tr into next tr, 3tr into last ch sp.

12th row: 12ch, 1tr into each of the 10th, 11th and 12th ch from hook, 1tr into first tr, 2ch, miss 2tr, 1tr, 2tr into next ch sp, 1tr into next tr, 8ch, miss 7 sts, 1tr, 8ch, 1tr into last tr, 7tr into next ch sp, 7tr into next ch sp, 1tr into next tr, (5ch, 2tr into next ch sp, 5ch, 1tr into 3rd dc, 1tr into 4th dc) 5 times, 5ch, 2tr into 5ch sp, 5ch, miss 3tr, 1tr into 4th tr, 7tr into next 5ch sp, 7tr into next ch sp, 1tr into next tr, 8ch, miss 5tr, 1tr, 8ch, miss 6tr, 1tr into next tr, 3tr into next ch sp, (5ch, 1tr into 3rd dc, 1tr into 4th dc, 5ch, 2tr into next ch sp) 3 times, 5ch, 1tr into 3rd dc, 1tr into 4th dc, 5ch, 6tr, 2ch, miss 2tr, 1tr, 2ch, 1tr into next tr, 2ch, 1gr into next gr, 5ch, 1dc into both ch of previous 2 rows, 5ch, 1gr into next gr, 2ch, 2tr.

13th row: 3ch, 1tr into 2nd tr, 2ch, 1gr into next gr, 8ch, 1gr into next gr, 2ch, 1tr into next tr, 2ch, 1tr into next tr, 2ch, 1tr into next tr, 2ch, miss 2tr, 5tr, (5ch, miss 2tr, 6dc) 3 times, 5ch, 7tr, 8ch, 1dc into next tr, 8ch, 13tr, 5ch, (6dc, 5ch, miss 2tr) 5 times, 6dc, 5ch, miss 2tr, 14tr, 8ch, 1dc into next tr, 8ch, 7tr, 2ch, miss 2tr, 1tr into 4th tr, 3tr into last ch sp.

14th row: 12ch, 1tr into each of the 10th, 11th and 12th ch from hook, 1tr into first tr, 2ch, miss 2tr, 10tr, 8ch, 1dc into next dc, 8ch, 11tr, (5ch, 2tr into next ch sp, 5ch, 1tr into 3rd dc, 1tr into 4th dc) 6 times, 5ch, 2tr into next ch sp, 5ch, miss 2tr, 11tr, 8ch, 1dc into next dc, 8ch, 10tr, (5ch, 1tr into 3rd dc, 1tr into 4th dc, 5ch, 2tr into next ch sp) 3 times, 5ch, miss 2tr, 6tr, 2ch, 1tr into next tr, 2ch, 1tr into next tr, 2ch, 1gr into next gr, 8ch, 1gr into next gr, 2ch, 2tr.

15th row: 3ch, 1tr into 2nd tr, 2ch, 1gr into next gr, 5ch, 1dc into both ch of 2 previous rows, 5ch, 1gr into next gr, 2ch, 1tr into next tr, 2ch, 7tr, 5ch, (6dc, 5ch, miss 2tr) twice, 6dc, 5ch, 13tr, *5ch, 1dc into all ch from 3 previous rows, 5ch, 1tr into next dc, 5ch, 1dc into all ch from 3 previous rows, 5ch*, 7tr, 5ch, (6dc, 5ch, miss 2tr) 6 times, 6dc, 5ch, miss 3tr, 8tr, rep from * to * once more, 13tr, 2ch, miss 2tr, 1tr, 3tr into next ch sp.

16th row: 12ch, 1tr into each of the 10th, 11th and 12th ch from hook, 1ch, 1tr into first tr, 2ch, miss 2 sts, 16tr, 5ch, 1tr into next tr, 5ch, 4tr, (5ch, 2tr into next ch sp, 5ch, 1tr into 3rd dc, 1tr into 4th dc) 7 times, 5ch, 2tr into next ch sp, 5ch, miss 3tr, 4tr, 5ch, 1tr into next tr, 5ch, 16tr, (5ch, 1tr into 3rd dc, 1tr into 4th dc, 5ch, 2tr into next ch sp) twice, 5ch, 1tr into 3rd dc, 1tr into 4th dc, 5ch, 6tr, 2ch, miss 2 sts, 1tr, 2ch, 1tr into next tr, 2ch, 1gr into next gr, 8ch, 1gr into next gr, 2ch, 2tr.

17th row: 3ch, 1tr into 2nd tr, 2ch, 1gr into next gr, 8ch, 1gr into next gr, 2ch, 1tr into next tr, 2ch, 1tr into next tr, 2ch, 1tr into next tr, 2ch, miss 2tr, 5tr, (5ch, miss 2tr, 6dc) twice, 5ch, 3tr into next ch sp, 1tr into next tr, 5ch, miss 6 sts, 1tr, 5ch, miss 7 sts, 1tr, 7tr into 5ch sp, 7tr into next 5ch sp, 1tr into next tr, 5ch, (6dc, 5ch, miss 2tr) 7 times, 6dc, 5ch, miss 3tr, 1tr into next tr, 7tr into next 5ch sp, 7tr into next 5ch sp, 1tr into next tr, 5ch, miss 6tr, 1tr, 5ch, miss 7tr, 1tr into next tr, 2tr into next 2ch sp, 1tr into next tr, 2ch, miss 2tr, 1tr, 3tr into last ch sp, 12ch, ss into base of last tr worked.

18th row: Ss into each of 12ch of the ch sp, 6ch, 1tr into 4th tr, 2tr into 2ch sp, 1tr into next tr, 2ch, miss 2tr, 1tr into next tr, 7tr into next 5ch sp, 7tr into next ch sp, 1tr into next tr, 8ch, miss 7tr, 1tr, 8ch, miss 6tr, 1tr, 3tr into next ch sp, (5ch, 1tr into 3rd dc, 1tr into 4th dc, 5ch, 2tr into next ch sp) 7 times, 5ch, 1tr into 3rd dc, 1tr into 4th dc, 5ch, 3tr into next ch sp, 1tr into next tr, 8ch, miss 6 sts, 1 tr, 8ch, miss 7 sts, 1tr, 7tr into 5ch sp, 7tr into next ch sp, 1tr into next tr, (5ch, 2tr into next ch sp, 5ch, 1tr into 3rd dc, 1tr into 4th dc) twice, 5ch, 2tr into next ch sp, 5ch, miss 2tr, 6tr, 2ch, 1tr into next tr, 2ch, 1tr into next tr, 2ch, 1gr into next gr, 5ch, 1dc into both ch of previous 2 rows, 5ch, 1gr into next gr, 2ch, 2tr.

19th row: 3ch, 1tr into 2nd tr, 2ch, 1gr into next gr, 8ch, 1gr into next gr, 2ch, 1tr into next tr, 2ch, 7tr, 5ch, (6dc, 5ch, miss 2tr) twice, 6dc, 5ch, miss 2tr, 14tr, 8ch, 1dc into next dc, 8ch, 7tr, 5ch, (6dc, 5ch, miss 2tr) 7 times, 7tr, 8ch, 1dc into next dc, 8ch, 13tr, 2ch, miss 2tr, 1tr, 2tr into next ch sp, 1tr into next tr, turn.

20th row: 6ch, 1tr into 4th tr, 2tr into next 2ch sp, 1tr into next tr, 2ch, miss 2 sts, 10tr, 8ch, 1dc into next dc, 8ch, 10tr, (5ch, 1tr into 3rd dc, 1tr into 4th dc, 5ch, 2tr into next ch sp) 6 times, 5ch, 1tr into 3rd dc, 1tr into 4th dc, 5ch, 10tr, 8ch, 1dc into next dc, 8ch, 11tr, (5ch, 2tr into next ch sp, 5ch, 1tr into 3rd dc, 1tr into 4th dc) 3 times, 5ch, 6tr, 2ch, miss 2 sts, 1tr into next tr, 2ch, 1tr into next tr, 2ch, 1gr into next gr, 8ch, 1gr into next gr, 2ch, 2tr.

21st row: 3ch, 1tr into 2nd tr, 2ch, 1gr into next gr, 5ch, 1dc into both ch of 2 previous rows, 5ch, 1gr into next gr, 2ch, 1tr into next tr, 2ch, 1tr into next tr, 2ch, 1tr into next tr, 2ch, miss 2 sts, 5tr, (5ch, miss 2tr, 6dc) twice, 5ch, miss 2tr, 6dc, 5ch, miss 3tr, 8tr, *5ch, 1dc into all ch of previous 3 rows, 5ch, 1tr into next tr, 5ch, 1dc into all ch of 3 previous rows, 5ch*, 13tr, 5ch, (miss 2 sts, 5ch, 6dc) 6 times, 13tr, rep from * to * once more, 7tr, 2ch, miss 2tr, 1tr into next tr, 2tr into next ch sp, 1tr into next tr, turn.

22nd row: 6ch, 1tr into 4th tr, 2tr into next 2ch sp, 1tr into next tr, 2ch, miss 2 sts, 4tr, 5ch, 1tr into next tr, 5ch, 16tr, (5ch, 1tr into 3rd dc, 1tr into 4th dc, 5ch, 2tr into next ch sp) 5 times, 5ch, 1tr into 3rd dc, 1tr into 4th dc, 5ch, 16tr, 5ch, 1tr into next tr, 5ch, 4tr, (5ch, 2tr into next ch sp, 5ch, 1tr into 3rd dc, 1tr into 4th dc) 3 times, 5ch, 2tr into next ch sp, 5ch, 6tr, 2ch, 1tr into next tr, 2ch, 1tr into next tr, 2ch, 1gr into next gr, 8ch, 1gr into next gr, 2ch, 2tr.

23rd row: 3ch, 1tr into 2nd tr, 2ch, 1gr into next gr, 8ch, 1gr into next gr, 2ch, 1tr into next tr, 2ch, 7tr, 5ch, (6dc, 5ch, miss 2tr) 3 times, 6dc, 5ch, miss 3tr, 1tr into next tr, 7tr into next 5ch sp, 7tr into next 5ch sp, 1tr into next tr, 8ch, miss 6 sts, 1tr, 8ch, miss 7 sts, 1tr into next tr, 3tr into next ch sp, 5ch, (6dc, 5ch, miss 2tr) 4 times, 6dc, 5ch, 3tr into next ch sp, 1tr into next tr, 8ch, miss 6 sts, 1tr, 8ch, miss 7 sts, 1tr into next tr, 7tr into next 5ch sp, 7tr into next 5ch sp, 1tr into next tr, 2ch, miss 2sts, 1tr into next tr, 2tr into next 2ch sp, 1tr into next tr, turn.

24th row: 6ch, 1tr into 4th tr, 2tr into next 2ch sp, 1tr into next tr, 2ch, miss 2tr, 13tr, *8ch, 1dc into next tr, 8ch*, 7tr, (5ch, 1tr into 3rd dc, 1tr into 4th dc, 5ch, 2tr into next ch sp) 4 times, 5ch, 1tr into 3rd dc, 1tr into 4th dc, 5ch, 7tr, rep from * to * once more, 13tr, (5ch, 2tr into next ch sp, 5ch, 1tr into 3rd dc, 1tr into 4th dc) 4 times, 5ch, 6tr, 2ch, miss 2 sts, 1tr, 2ch, 1tr into next tr, 2ch, 1gr into next gr, 5ch, 1dc into both ch of previous 2 rows, 5ch, 1gr into next gr, 2ch, 2tr.

25th row: 3ch, 1tr into 2nd tr, 2ch, 1gr into next gr, 8ch, 1gr into next gr, 2ch, 1tr into next tr, 2ch, 1tr into next tr, 2ch, 1tr into next tr, 2ch, miss

2tr, 5tr, (5ch, miss 2tr, 6dc) 4 times, 5ch, miss 2tr, 11tr, 8ch, 1dc into next dc, 8ch, 10tr, 5ch, (miss 2tr, 5ch, 6dc) 4 times, 5ch, miss 2tr, 10tr, 8ch, 10tr, 2ch, miss 2 sts, 1tr into next tr, 2tr into next 2ch sp, 1tr into next tr, turn.

26th row: 6ch, 1tr into 4th tr, 2tr into 2ch sp, 1tr into next tr, 2ch, miss 2 sts, 7tr, *5ch, 1dc into all ch of previous 3 rows, 5ch, 1tr into next dc, 5ch, 1dc into all ch of previous 3 rows, 5ch*, 13tr, (5ch, 1tr into 3rd dc, 1tr into 4th dc, 5ch, 2tr into next ch sp) 3 times, 5ch, 1tr into 3rd dc, 1tr into 4th dc, 5ch, 13tr, rep from * to * once more, 7tr, (5ch, 2tr into next ch sp, 5ch, 1tr into 3rd dc, 1tr into 4th dc) 4 times, 5ch, 2tr into next ch sp, 5ch, 5tr, 2ch, 1tr into next tr, 2ch, 1tr into next tr, 2ch, 1gr into next gr, 8ch, 1gr into next gr, 2ch, 2tr.

27th row: 3ch, 1tr into 2nd tr, 2ch, 1gr into next gr, 5ch, 1dc into both ch of previous 2 rows, 5ch, 1gr into next gr, 2ch, 1tr into next tr, 2ch, 7tr, 5ch, (6dc, 5ch, miss 2tr) 4 times, 6dc, 5ch, miss 3tr, 4tr, 5ch, 1tr into next tr, 5ch, 15tr, (5ch, miss 2tr, 6dc) 3 times, 5ch, miss 2tr, 15tr, 5ch, 1tr into next tr, 5ch, 4tr, 2ch, miss 2 sts, 1tr, 2tr into next ch sp, 1tr into next tr, turn.

28th row: 6ch, 1tr into 4th tr, 2tr into next 2ch sp, 1tr into next tr, 2ch, miss 2 sts, 1tr, 7tr into next ch sp, 7tr into next ch sp, 1tr into next tr, *8ch, miss 6ch, 1tr into next tr, 8ch, miss 6 sts, 1tr into next tr*, 3tr into next ch sp, (5ch, 1tr into 3rd dc, 1tr into 4th dc, 5ch, 2tr into next ch sp) twice, 5ch, 1tr into 3rd dc, 1tr into 4th dc, 5ch, 3tr into next ch sp, 1tr into next tr, rep from * to * once more, 7tr into next ch sp, 7tr into next ch sp, 1tr into next tr, (5ch, 2tr into next ch sp, 5ch, 1tr into 3rd dc, 1tr into 4th dc) 5 times, 5ch, 6tr, 2ch, miss 2 sts, 1tr, 2ch, 1tr into next tr, 2ch, 1gr into next gr, 8ch, 1gr into next gr, 2ch, 2tr.

29th row: 3ch, 1tr into 2nd tr, 2ch, 1gr into next gr, 8ch, 1gr into next gr, 2ch, 1tr into next tr, 2ch, 1tr into next tr, 2ch, 1tr into next tr, 2ch, miss 2 sts, 5tr, (5ch, miss 2tr, 6dc) 5 times, 5ch, miss 2tr, 14tr, 8ch, 1dc into next dc, 8ch, 7tr, (5ch, miss 2tr, 6dc) twice, 5ch, miss 2tr, 7tr, 8ch, 1dc into next dc, 8ch, 13tr, 2ch, miss 2 sts, 1tr into next tr, 2tr into next 2ch sp, 1tr into next tr, turn.

30th row: 6ch, 1tr into 4th tr, 2tr into next 2ch sp, 1tr into next tr, 2ch, miss 2 sts, *10tr, 8ch, 1dc into next dc, 8ch, 10tr*, 5ch, 1tr into 3rd dc, 1tr into 4th dc, 5ch, miss 2tr, 5ch, 1tr into 3rd dc, 1tr into 4th dc, 5ch, rep from * to * once more, (5ch, 2tr into next ch sp, 5ch, 1tr into 3rd dc, 1tr into 4th dc) 5 times, 5ch, 2tr into next ch sp, 5ch, miss 2tr, 6tr, 2ch, 1tr into next tr, 2ch, 1tr into next tr, 2ch, 1gr into next gr, 5ch, 1dc into both ch of previous 2 rows, 5ch, 1gr into next gr, 2ch, 2tr.

31st row: 3ch, 1tr into 2nd tr, 2ch, 1gr into next gr, 8ch, 1gr into next gr, 2ch, 1tr into next tr, 2ch, 7tr, 5ch, (6dc, 5ch, miss 2tr) 5 times, 6dc, 5ch, miss 3tr, 7tr, *5ch, 1dc into all ch of previous 3 rows, 5ch, 1tr into next dc,

5ch, 1dc into all ch of previous 3 rows, 5ch*, 13tr, 5ch, miss 2tr, 6dc, 5ch, miss 2tr, 13tr, rep from * to * once more, 7tr, 2ch, miss 2sts, 1tr into next tr, 2tr into next 2ch sp, 1tr into next tr, turn.

32nd row: 6ch, 1tr into 4th tr, 2tr into next 2ch sp, 1tr into next tr, 2ch, miss 2 sts, 4tr, 5ch, 1tr into next tr, 5ch, 16tr, 5ch, 1tr into 3rd dc, 1tr into 4th dc, 5ch, 16tr, 5ch, 1tr into next tr, 5ch, 4tr, (5ch, 2tr into next ch sp, 5ch, 1tr into 3rd dc, 1tr into 4th dc) 6 times, 5ch, 6tr, 2ch, miss 2tr, 1tr into next tr, 2ch, 1tr into next tr, 2ch, 1gr into next gr, 8ch, 1gr into next gr, 2ch, 2tr.

33rd row: 3ch, 1tr into 2nd tr, 2ch, 1gr into next gr, 5ch, 1dc into both ch of previous 2 rows, 5ch, 1gr into next gr, 2ch, 1tr into next tr, 2ch, 1tr into next tr, 2ch, 1tr into next tr, 2ch, miss 2tr, 5tr, (5ch, miss 2tr, 6dc) 6 times, 5ch, 1tr into 4th tr, 7tr into 5ch sp, 1tr into next tr, 5ch, miss 7 sts, 1tr, 5ch, miss 6 sts, 1tr, 3tr into next ch sp, 5ch, 3tr into next ch sp, 1tr into next tr, 5ch, miss 7 sts, 1tr, 5ch, miss 6 sts, 1tr, 7tr into next 5ch sp, 7tr into next 5ch sp, 1tr into next tr, 2ch, miss 2tr, 1tr, 2tr into next 2ch sp, 1tr into next tr, turn.

Rep from 2nd to 33rd rows until border is sufficiently long to go round three edges of the bedspread, plus fullness for the two corners.

Outside edging

On the outer edge join in yarn to first sp, *7dc into sp, 1dc into end of row without sp*, rep from * to * all along edge of border but working 12dc into sp at points of zig-zag.

Inside edging

Join in yarn at straight edge, *yrh 3 times, insert hook into 3ch sp at beg of a row, yrh and draw loop through, yrh, draw through 2 loops, yrh, draw through next 2 loops, yrh, insert hook into border st of next row, yrh and draw loop through, (yrh, draw through 2 loops) 4 times, 3ch, yrh, insert hook between previous 2 sts, yrh and draw loop through, (yrh, draw through 2 loops) twice, rep from * all along edge.

To make up: Starch lightly and press on the wrong side. Sew border to bedspread.

Target rag rug (See opposite)

Whether you want to use up scraps of fabric, or get the dye pot on the boil, this rag rug worked in bold, rich colours is a contemporary adaptation of an old-fashioned idea. The rug measures about 45 in. in diameter but the size can be adjusted to suit yourself. You will need:

2 in. wide strips of cotton fabric (see below).
A No 7·00 crochet hook.

Tension
Pull each crochet loop out to measure about 1 in. The first 3 completed rows should make a round of about 4½ in. in diameter.

Working in rag
The strips of cloth need not be of any particular length; new pieces are joined in as required. To save stitching pieces together or having to sew in ends later, simply lay both ends—the nearly finished one and the new one—along the top of the stitches about to be worked. Continue with the new strip, working over the two ends and into the previous row in the usual way.

1st round: Using No 7·00 hook, make 6ch. Join with ss to first ch to form a ring.

2nd round: Make 10dc into ring.

3rd round: Make 2dc into each dc. 20dc.

4th round: *2dc into first dc, 1dc into each of next 2dc, rep from * to end.

5th–31st rounds: As 4th. Fasten off.

To follow the colour scheme illustrated
If preferred, strips can be made from old white cotton sheets. To copy the colours illustrated, use DYLON hot water dyes: Black 8, Honey Tan 45, Wine

Target rag rug (see opposite and page 136)

43 and Cerise 44 (equal parts mixed make Brilliant Pink), Coffee 7 and Havana Brown 5 (equal parts mixed make Rich Dark Brown).

Work colour sequence as follows:

1st–5th rows: Brilliant Pink.
6th and 7th rows: White.
8th row: Honey Tan.
9th and 10th rows: Rich Dark Brown.
11th row: Black.
12th and 13th rows: White.
14th and 15th rows: Honey Tan.
16th–18th rows: Rich Dark Brown.
19th row: Black.
20th and 21st rows: White.
22nd–24th rows: Honey Tan.
25th–28th rows: Rich Dark Brown.
29th row: Black.
30th row: White.
31st row: Brilliant Pink.

Note: Using either random-coloured rags or the set colour sequence, the rug can be made larger or smaller, as required.

Mother and daughter dresses (See pages 138 - 41)

Filet crochet is used to work these matching dresses for mother and daughter. There is a simple chart for the diamond motifs on page 143. A scalloped hem makes the perfect finishing touch. The mother's dress fits a 34 in. bust and measures 37 in. in length; the daughter's dress fits a 26 in. chest and measures 26 in. in length. You will need:

For the mother's dress, *Twilley's Lyscordet:* 20 balls.
A zip fastener measuring 14 in.
A No 2·50 crochet hook.
For the daughter's dress, *Twilley's Lyscordet:* 10 balls.

Tension

4 sps (8 sts) and 3 rows to 1 in.

Mother's dress back

Using No 2·50 hook, make 209ch.

1st row: 1tr into 4th ch from hook, *1ch, miss 1ch, work 6tr into next st, take hook out of loop, insert hook from front to back into the top loop of the first of these 6tr, catch the loose loop and draw it through, fasten with 1ch (called 1 popcorn st), 1ch, miss 1ch, 1tr into next ch, rep from * to end. 103 sps.

2nd row: 4ch to count as first tr and 1ch, *1tr in popcorn st, 1ch, 1 popcorn st in tr (when working popcorn st on WS rows always insert hook into first tr from back to front), 1ch, rep from * to end, 1tr into 3rd of 4ch.

Continue as now set; working from patt chart and working from centre of rep as indicated. Work rows 1 to 52, then rep rows 19 to 52 throughout,

Next row: Patt over first 4 sps, turn. Fasten off. Return to where work was left, miss first sp in centre and rejoin yarn. Patt to end. Complete to match first side, reversing shapings.

Mother's dress front
Work as given for Back, but omitting centre back opening, until work measures the same as Back to armholes.

Shape armholes
Next row: Ss over first 4 sps, patt to end.
Next row: Patt to last 2 sps, turn. Dec one sp at armhole edge on each of next 2 rows. 31 sps. Continue without shaping until armhole measures 8 in., ending at armhole edge.

Shape neck and shoulder
Next row: Patt to last 10 sps, turn.
Next row: Ss over first 3 sps, patt to last 4 sps, turn.
Next row: Ss over first 4 sps, patt to last 2 sps, turn.
Next row: Patt over first 4 sps, turn. Fasten off. Return to where work was left, miss first sp in centre and rejoin yarn. Patt to end. Complete to match first side, reversing shapings.

Mother's dress front
Work as given for Back, but omitting centre back opening, until work measures the same as Back to armholes.

Shape armholes
Next row: Ss over first 4 sps, patt to last 4 sps, turn.
Next row: Ss over first 2 sps, patt to last 2 sps, turn. Dec one sp at each end of each of next 2 rows. 63 sps. Continue without shaping until armholes measure 5 in.

Shape neck
Next row: Patt over first 21 sps, turn. Dec one sp at neck edge on each of next 5 rows. Continue without shaping until armhole measures same as Back, ending at armhole edge.

Shape shoulder
Next row: Ss over first 4 sps, patt to end.
Next row: Patt to last 4 sps, turn. Rep the first of these 2 rows once more. Fasten off. Return to where work was left, miss 21 sps in centre and rejoin yarn. Patt to end. Complete to match first side, reversing shapings.

To make up
Press pieces with a warm iron, under a damp cloth, taking care not to flatten the popcorns. Join shoulder seams. With right side facing, work one row dc round neck edge.

Mother and daughter dresses (see pages 136–141)

Next row: *1tr, 1ch, 1 popcorn st, 1ch, rep from * to end, finishing with 1tr.

Next row: As previous row but alternating the popcorns. Fasten off. Work in the same way round armholes. Join side seams. Work round lower

Fringed poncho (see pages 142–143)

edge starting from one side seam and with right side facing, join in yarn, 4ch, 1 popcorn st into first tr, *1ch, 1tr into next popcorn st, 1ch, 1 popcorn st into next tr, rep from * once more, turn.

Next row: 4ch, 1 popcorn st in tr, 1tr in popcorn st, 1 popcorn st in tr, turn.

Next row: 4ch, 1 popcorn st in tr. Fasten off. Rejoin yarn to next tr along lower edge and continue in the same way all round. Sew in zip. Press seams.

Daughter's dress

Back and front are worked in the same way. First work the back. Using No 2·50 hook, make 141ch.

1st row: 1tr in 4th ch from hook, *1ch, miss 1ch, 1 popcorn st in next ch, 1ch, miss 1ch, 1tr in next ch, rep from * to end. 69 sps.

2nd row: 4ch to count as first tr and ch, *1tr in popcorn st, 1ch, 1 popcorn st in tr, 1ch, rep from * to end, 1tr in top of turning ch. Continue as set, working from patt chart and working from centre of rep as indicated.

Work to row 42, then omit the motifs but continue to work the popcorn sts to row 52, then continue in filet crochet (ie, 1 sp, 1tr alternately) throughout *at the same time* dec one sp at each end of 12th and every following 6th row until 55 sps rem. Continue without shaping until work measures $17\frac{1}{2}$ in. from beginning.

Shape armholes

Next row: Ss over first 4 sps, patt to last 4 sps, turn. Dec one sp at each end of each of next 3 rows. 41 sps. Continue without shaping until armhole measures 4 in.

Shape neck

Next row: Patt over first 12 sps, turn. Dec one sp at neck edge on each of next 3 rows. Continue without shaping until armhole measures $5\frac{1}{2}$ in. Fasten off.

Return to where work was left, miss 17 sps in centre and rejoin yarn. Work to end. Complete to match first side, reversing shapings.

To make up

Press work with a warm iron under a damp cloth. Join shoulder seams. With right side facing, work 1 row dc round neck edge, then 1 row popcorn sts as on mother's dress. Work in same way round armholes. Join side seams.

Work round lower edge as given for 2nd row for 9 rows, alternating the popcorn sts. Work points as given for mother's dress. Press seams.

KEY

← BLOCK   ← POPCORN   ← SPACE

51
41
31
21
11
1
34 SPACE
REPEAT
BEGIN HERE

Fringed poncho (See page 139)

This bright, cheerful version of the endlessly useful poncho is made out of 140 squares and is quick and easy to make. It measures 12 squares by 12 squares (flat), i.e., 56 in. square, including the fringing. To make it you will need:

For the poncho, *Lee Target Motoravia Double Knitting Wool:* 12 oz red; 12 oz turquoise; 6 oz navy.

A No 3·50 crochet hook.

For the fringing and making up, 9 oz red.

A piece of cardboard 4½ in. deep and about 4 in. long.

A No 3·00 crochet hook.

Tension

Each square measures 4 in. across.

Bedspread and rug (see opposite and pages 144–145)

Square
Using No 3·50 hook and turquoise, make 5ch and join into ring with ss.

1st round: 3ch to count as first dtr, 2dtr into ring, (1ch, 3dtr into ring) 3 times, 1ch, ss to top of last 3ch. Fasten off.

2nd round: Join navy to a 1ch sp, (3ch, 2dtr, 1ch, 3dtr) all into same sp, *1ch, (3dtr, 1ch, 3dtr) all into next sp, rep from * twice more, 1ch, ss to top of first 3ch. Fasten off.

3rd round: Join in turquoise to 1ch corner sp, (3ch, 2dtr, 1ch, 3dtr) all into same sp, *1ch, 3dtr in next sp, 1ch, (3dtr, 1ch, 3dtr) all into corner sp, rep from * twice more, 1ch, 3dtr in next sp, 1ch, ss to top of first 3ch. Fasten off.

4th round: Join red to corner sp, (3ch, 2dtr, 1ch, 3dtr) all in same sp, *(1ch, 3dtr in next sp) twice, 1ch, (3dtr, 1ch, 3dtr) all into corner sp, rep from * twice more, (1ch, 3dtr in 1ch sp) twice, 1ch, ss to top of first 3ch. Fasten off. Make 140 squares in all.

To make up
Darn in all ends and press squares on wrong side. Sew together (wrong sides together and oversew loosely) in a square 12 by 12, leaving 4 squares out of centre. Crochet 4 rows round neck, using No 3·00 hook and red as follows:

1st round: *3dtr into sp, 1ch, rep from * all round.

2nd–4th rounds: Work one st into each dc, dec one st at each corner.

To fringe
Wind red wool round the piece of cardboard eight times (this gives 16 fringe lengths) and break wool. Slide wool off card and knot through each space in crocheted edge of big square. Cut loops through and trim.

Bedspread and rug (See opposite and pages 144–145)

Boldly contrasting colours combine in this matching bedspread and rug for a dramatic effect. The motifs for the bedspread are worked in single yarn, the rug motifs in double yarn. The bedspread measures approximately 54 in. by 68 in. and the rug approximately 60 in. by 48 in. You will need:

For the bedspread, Lister Lavenda Double Knitting: 30 oz brown, A; 15 oz green, B; 15 oz white, C.
A No 3·50 crochet hook.
For the rug: 46 oz brown, A; 23 oz green, B; 23 oz white, C.
A No 5·50 crochet hook.

Tension
Bedspread: Motif measures $4\frac{1}{2}$ in. worked with No 3·50 hook and single yarn.
Rug: Motif measures 6 in. worked with No 5·50 hook and double yarn.

Bedspread

D	C	A	D	A	D	C	A	D	C	A	D
C	A	D	A	D	C	A	D	C	A	D	B
A	D	A	D	C	A	D	C	A	D	B	C
D	A	D	C	A	D	C	A	D	B	C	D
A	D	C	A	D	C	A	D	B	C	D	A
C	A	D	C	A	D	B	C	D	A	C	D
A	D	C	A	D	B	C	D	A	C	D	B
D	C	A	D	B	C	D	A	C	D	B	C
C	A	D	B	C	D	A	C	D	B	C	D
A	D	B	C	D	A	C	D	B	C	D	B
D	B	C	D	A	C	D	B	C	D	B	C
B	C	D	A	C	D	B	C	D	B	C	D
C	D	A	C	D	B	C	D	B	C	D	A
D	A	C	D	B	C	D	B	C	D	A	C

Rug

B	D	C	D	B	C	D	A
D	C	D	B	C	D	A	D
C	D	B	C	D	A	D	C
D	B	C	D	A	D	C	A
B	C	D	A	D	C	A	D
C	D	A	D	C	A	D	B
D	A	D	C	A	D	B	C
A	D	C	A	D	B	C	A
D	C	A	D	B	C	A	D
C	A	D	B	C	A	D	B

Bedspread

Large motif

Using No 3·50 hook and single yarn throughout, make 4ch. Join with ss to form a ring.

1st round: 2ch to count as first htr, 17htr into ring, join with ss to second of 2ch. 18 sts.

2nd round: 2ch, 1htr in next st, 2htr in next st, *1htr in each of next 2 sts, 2htr in next st, rep from * to end, join with ss to 2nd of 2ch. Break off first colour. 24 sts.

3rd round: Join in second colour to ss, 2ch, work to end as 2nd round. Break off second colour. 32 sts.

4th round: Join in third colour, 3ch, 1tr in each of next 2 sts, 2tr in next st, *1tr in each of next 3 sts, 2tr in next st, rep from * to end, join with ss to 3rd of 3ch. 40 sts.

5th round: Using 3rd colour, as 4th round. 50 sts. Fasten off. Work motifs as follows:

Motif A: 1st colour A, 2nd colour B, 3rd colour C. Make 40.
Motif B: 1st colour B, 2nd colour A, 3rd colour C. Make 25.
Motif C: 1st colour C, 2nd colour A, 3rd colour B. Make 53.
Motif D: 1st colour C, 2nd colour B, 3rd colour A. Make 62.

Small motif

1st and 2nd rounds: Using No 3·50 hook and A, work as 1st and 2nd rounds of Large Motif. Fasten off. Make 154 small motifs.

Rug

Using No 5·50 hook and yarn double throughout, work motifs as for bedspread. Make 18 Motif A, 12 Motif B, 21 Motif C, 29 Motif D and 63 small motifs using A.

To make up

Press all pieces under a damp cloth, using a warm iron. Following the appropriate chart, join the large motifs first, then sew the small motifs between. Press as before.

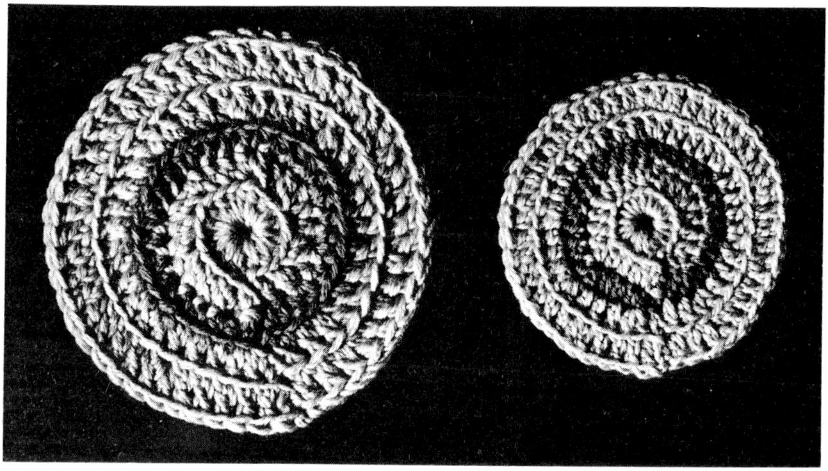

Details of the motifs used in the matching bedspread and rug set (see page 143 and opposite)

10 CROCHET STITCHES

The first step

To place the yarn on the hook, make a slip knot in the yarn (a) and tighten it round the hook in its curve (b, c). There is a flat bar in the centre of the hook and it is this part which is held in the thumb and forefinger of the right hand. The second finger rests against the hook to control it, at the same time keeping the loop in its correct position on the hook.

The yarn is controlled by the left hand in the following way. Wind the end of the yarn round the little finger, across the palm and through between the second and third fingers (d). The thumb and forefinger holds the knot of the last stitch made just under the hook (e). As each new stitch is made, the thumb and forefinger move to the new knot (f).

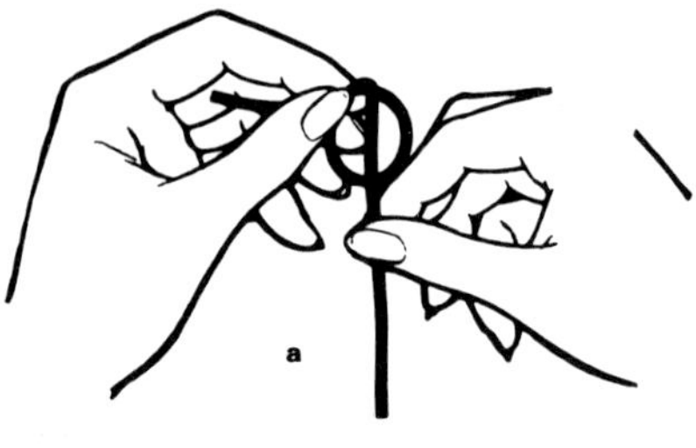
a

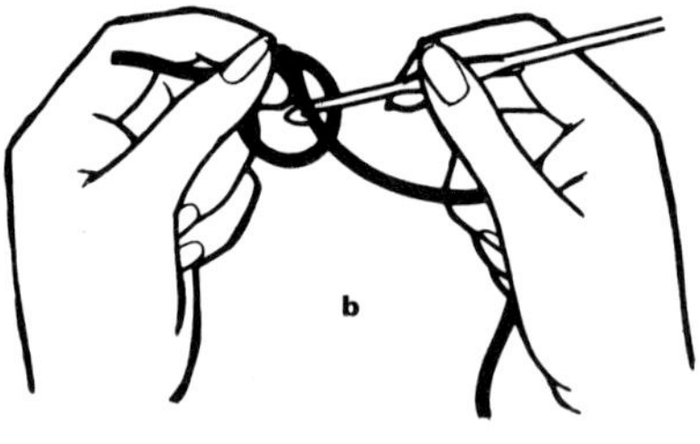
b

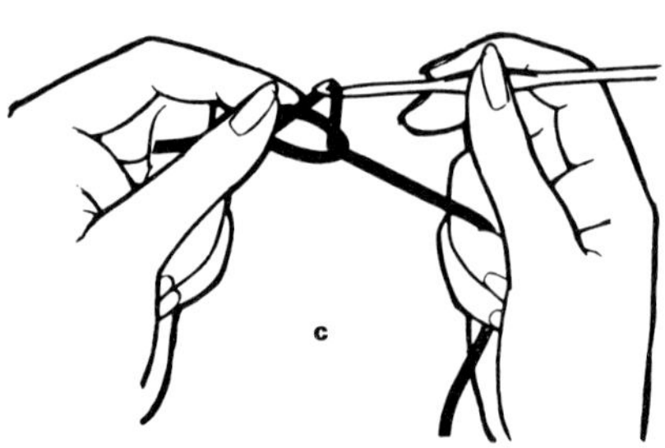
c

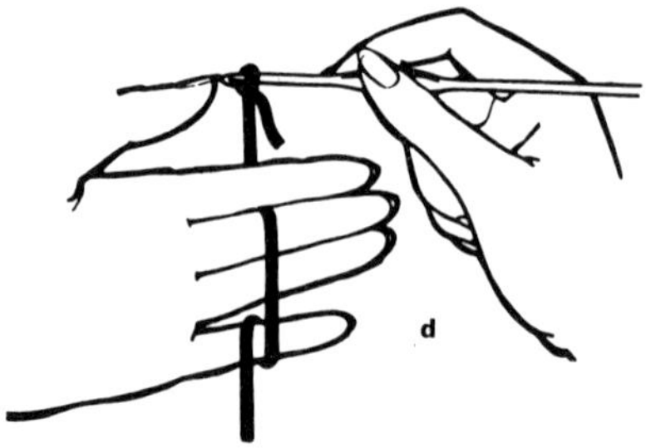
d

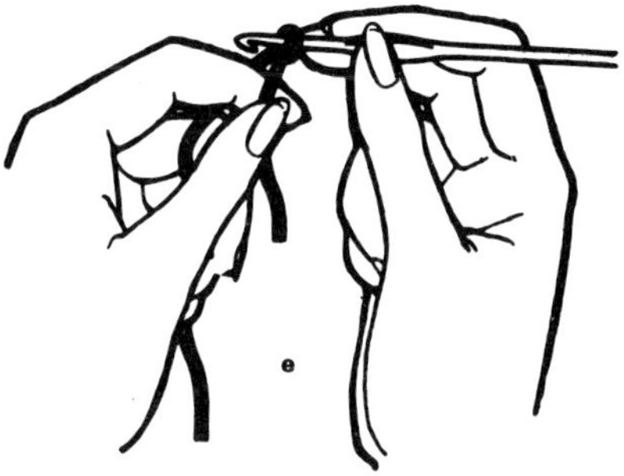

e

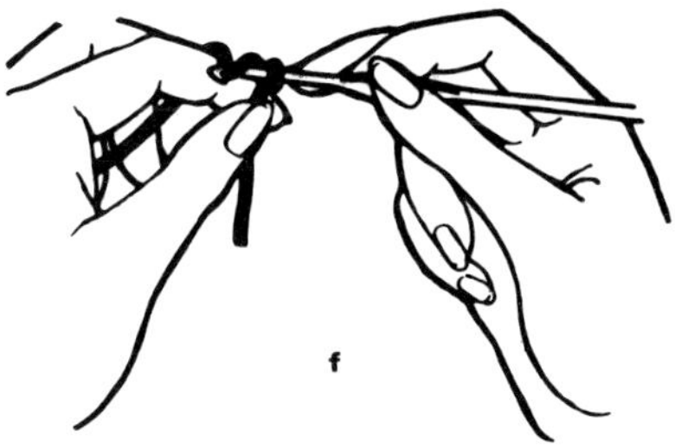

f

g

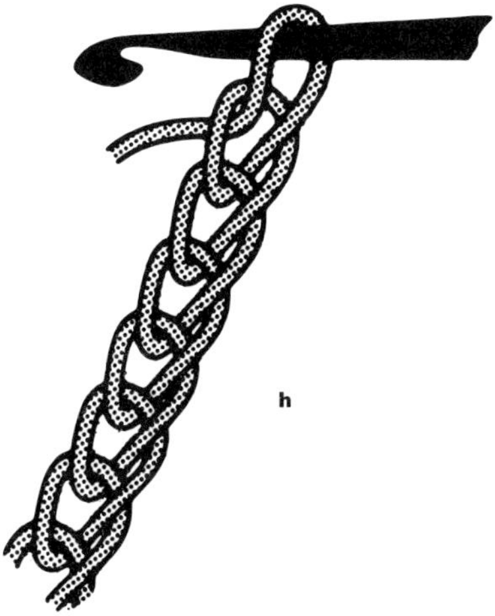

h

Chain stitch
Put the yarn over the hook, catching it in the curve (g). Pull the yarn through the loop already on the hook. This forms the next chain stitch (h) and usually a number of these chains forms the foundation or start of a piece of crochet.

Turning chain
Chain stitches are also used at the ends of rows. Because crochet stitches have depth and are worked from the top, it is first necessary to take the work up to the correct level by using chain stitches. The number of chain depends on the depth of the stitch to follow. For double crochet, one turning chain; half treble, 2; treble, 3; double treble, 4; triple treble, 5; quadruple treble, 6.

Slip stitch
Insert hook into stitch, put yarn round the hook and draw the loop through both stitch and loop already on hook (i, overleaf). This forms a flat stitch with no depth and therefore no turning chain are required. It can be used to give a firm edge, for joining the beginning of the work to the end when working in rounds or simply to take the yarn to a certain

part of the work without adding any dimension.

Double crochet
Insert the hook into the stitch, put the yarn over the hook (j) and draw the loop through so that there are two loops on the hook (k). Put the yarn over the hook and draw the loop through both loops (l).

Half treble
Yarn round hook (m), insert hook into next stitch, yarn round hook and draw loop through so that there are three loops on the hook (n), yarn round hook and draw through all three loops (o).

Treble
Yarn round hook (p), insert the hook into the next stitch, yarn round hook and pull loop through so that there are three loops on the hook (q). Yarn round hook and pull through two of the loops, thus leaving two loops on the hook (r). Yarn round hook and draw through the remaining two loops (s).

Double treble
Yarn round hook twice, insert hook into the next stitch, yarn round hook and draw loop through so that there are four loops on the hook (t). Yarn round hook and draw through two loops (three loops on hook), yarn round hook and draw through two loops (two loops on hook), yarn round hook and draw through remaining two loops.

Triple treble
Yarn round hook three times, insert hook into the next stitch and draw loop through so that there are five

i

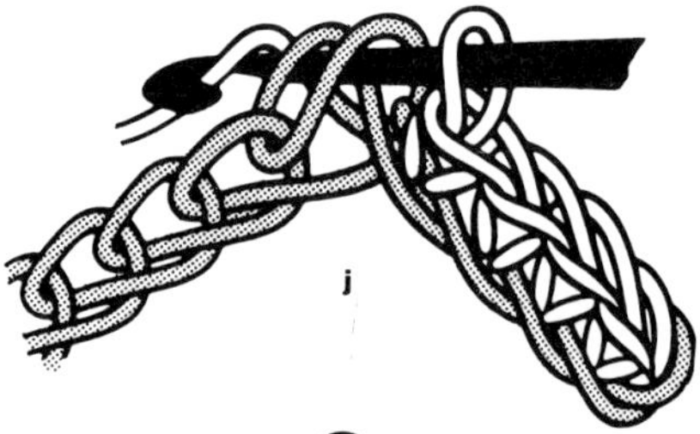
j

k

l

m

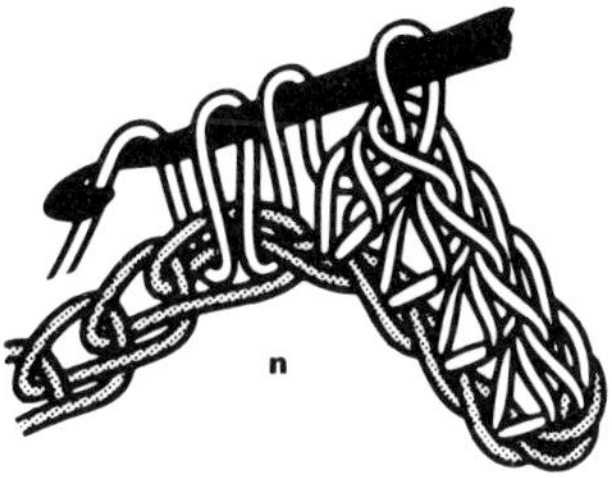
n

o

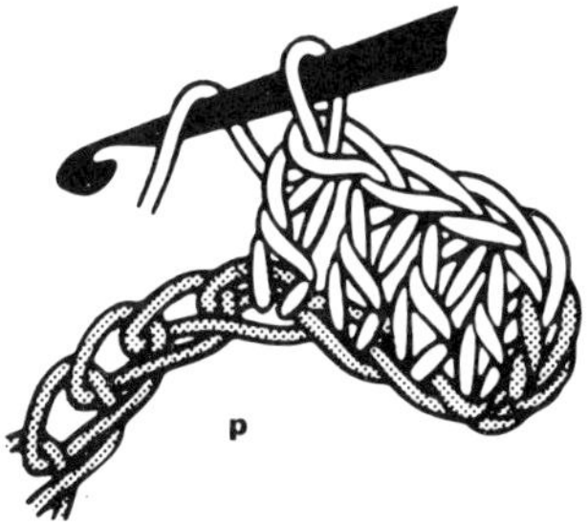
p

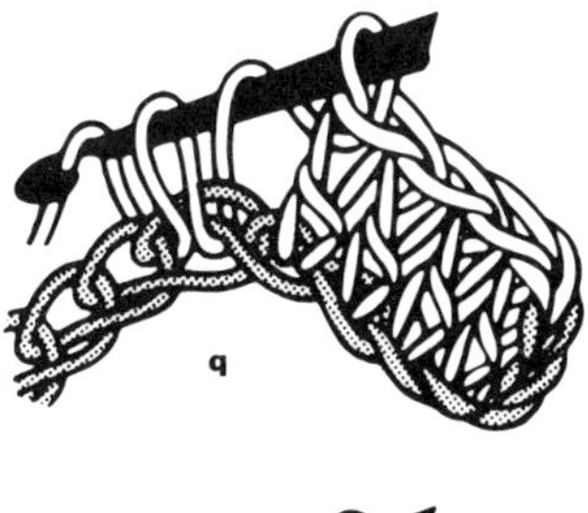
q

r

s

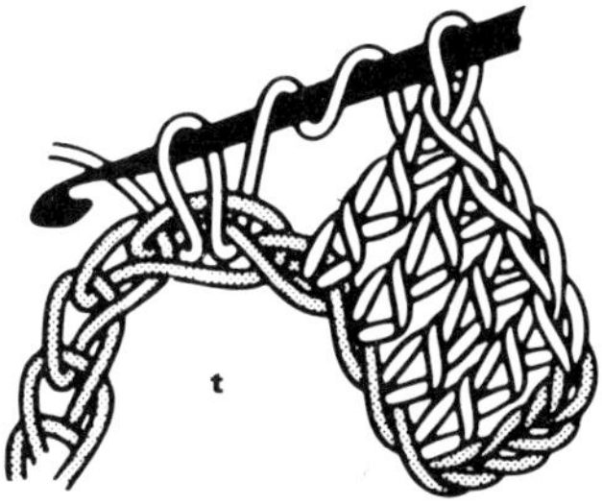
t

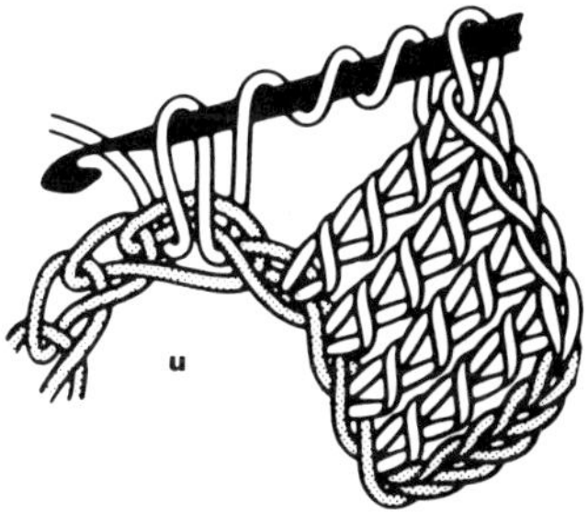
u

loops on the hook (u). Yarn round hook and draw through two loops (four loops on hook), yarn round hook and draw through two loops (three loops on hook), yarn round hook and draw through two loops (two loops on hook), yarn round hook and draw through remaining two loops.

Quadruple treble

Yarn round hook four times, insert hook into the next stitch and draw the loop through, making six loops on the hook (v, overleaf). Yarn round hook and draw through two loops (five loops on hook), yarn round hook and draw through two loops (four loops on hook), yarn round hook and draw through two loops (three loops on hook), yarn round hook and draw through two loops (two loops on hook), yarn round hook and draw through remaining two loops.

Directions of working
Crochet can be worked in straight rows, travelling backwards and forwards with turning chain used at the beginning of each row (w). Alternatively crochet can be worked in the round, starting with a circle of chain joined by a slip stitch (xa, b). The work continues round into the circle, gradually building out.

Filet crochet
Although crochet can be worked into a solid fabric or into a lacy open type of work, there is one distinctive form of the craft which is built up entirely of blocks and spaces worked in straight rows. The blocks are positioned to form any motif pattern. Spaces are made by missing several stitches, working one chain for each stitch missed and dividing the spaces with one treble. To make a block, several treble are worked before the next space (y). Instructions often take the form of charts with crosses representing the blocks and a key gives the number of stitches per block.

Increasing
As a general rule, patterns give detailed instructions for shaping. Usually this is achieved by working several times into the one stitch. Occasionally, especially when working an openwork pattern in the round, the number of chain loops is increased. It is possible, too, to

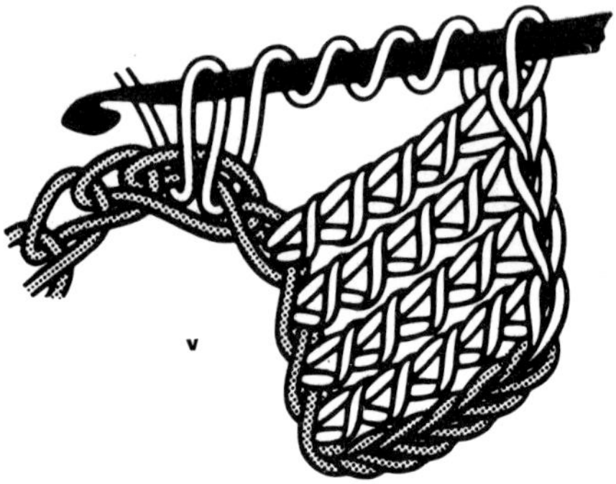
v

w

xa

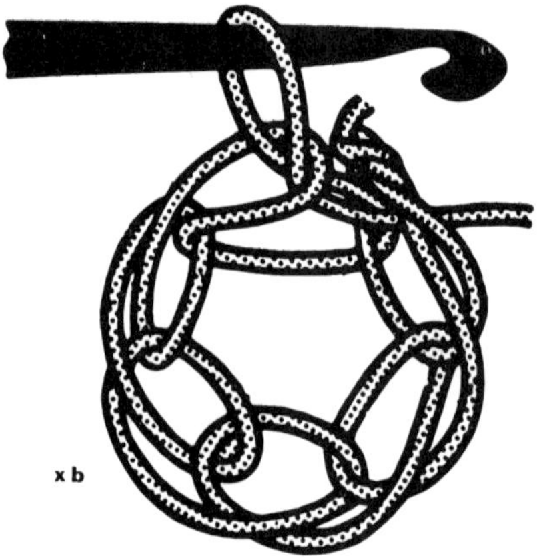
xb

y

z

increase simply by using a larger size of hook.

Decreasing
These, too, are usually given in pattern instructions and methods are to omit a stitch, to work two stitches together by not completing the final stage of either and then working them simultaneously or by leaving stitches unworked. The crochet hook can also be changed to a smaller size.

Measuring tension
To check that your tension is the same as that required by the pattern, work a square of about four inches by four inches using the suggested size of hook. Press as given at the end of the instructions and then using a rigid rule, measure across and down one inch, marking the positions with pins. To find the tension count the number of rows and stitches between the pins. If the numbers are higher than given in the pattern, the work is too tight and a larger hook must be used. Similarly, if there are too few stitches and rows, the work is too slack and a smaller hook is required.

Joining in new yarn
If possible, avoid making knots in the work. When there is about six in. of the old yarn left, lay the new end along the top of the stitches being worked and continue with the old yarn until there is about three inches left. Then lay the old yarn along the top of the next stitches and work over it with the new yarn. When working in chain, work with double thread for about three inches.

Finishing off
At the end of the work, cut the yarn to about six in., draw the end through the last loop and pull tight. Darn in this and any other ends on the back of the work using a blunt-ended needle.

Picots
Make a chain of three to five stitches, depending on how large a picot is required, then make a ring by working a double crochet or a slip stitch into the first chain (z). This can be used to make a decorative edging or to add detail in a lacy pattern.

Blocking out
Sometimes crochet requires to be blocked out and always when the work is very open. In effect, the work has shrunk in whilst being crocheted and must be pinned out to the correct shape and measurements, usually before sewing up.

Always work on a clean, flat surface and use rustless dressmaking pins. Following the correct measurements, draw out the correct shape on a sheet of white paper. Pin the crochet onto this, first pinning the edges and then pin each picot, loop or space into position. Cover with a damp cloth and leave until the cloth is absolutely dry.

Making up

Seams can be made with either back stitch, overcasting or by crocheting a line of slip stitch through the double thickness of the two pieces placed right sides together.

Always follow pressing instructions carefully. With some man-made fibres, pressing is not recommended because the fabric can stretch by several inches and lose its texture for ever.

Left handed workers

It is possible to learn crochet by reading left for right and right for left. Any diagrams can be followed by looking at them in a mirror. However, it is often possible to approach something completely new by following the instructions exactly as given as if you were right-handed rather than making it unnecessarily complicated.

CHART ENLARGEMENTS

Cross stitch napkins (see page 19)

Above: *Cross stitch napkins* (see page 19); right: another of the motifs

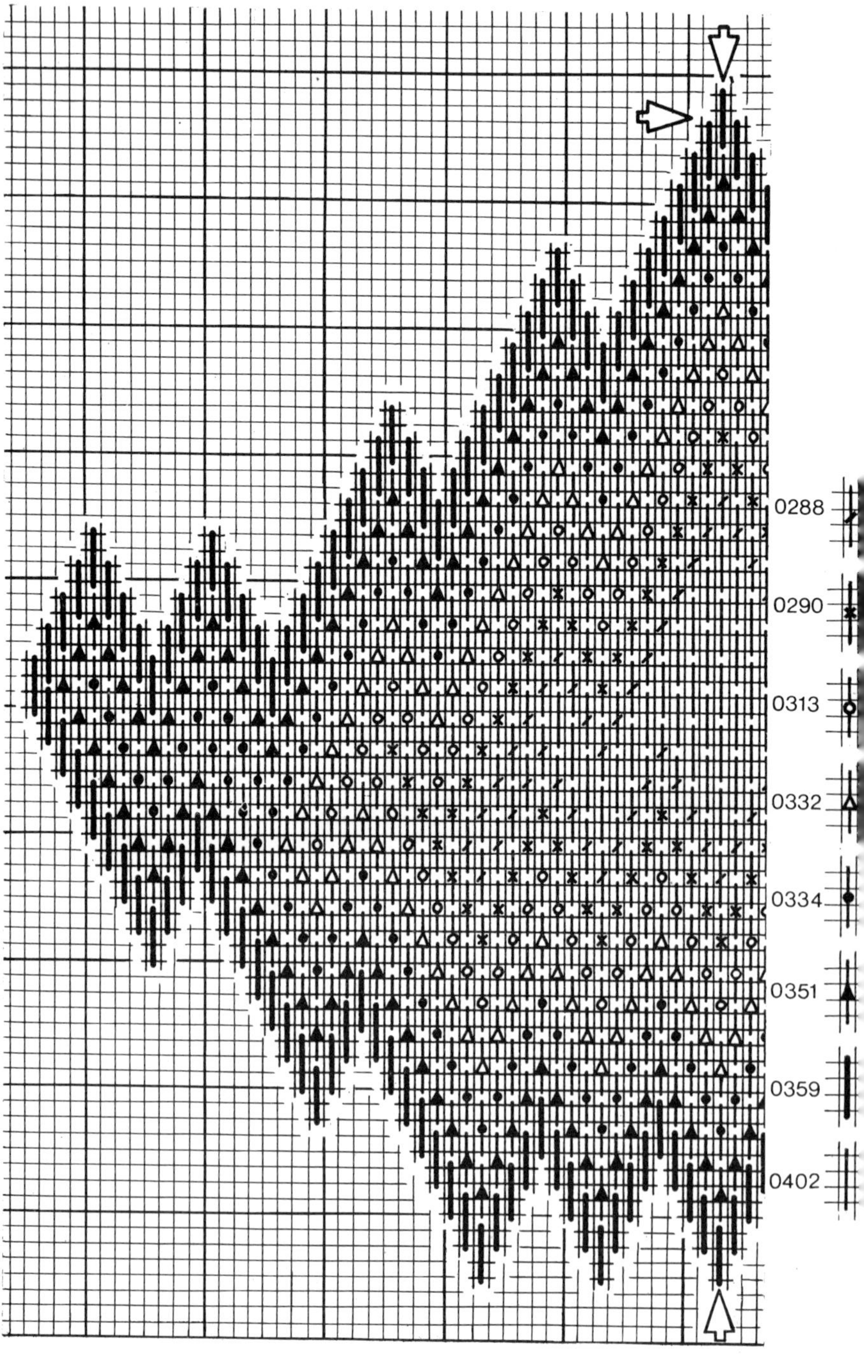
0288
0290
0313
0332
0334
0351
0359
0402

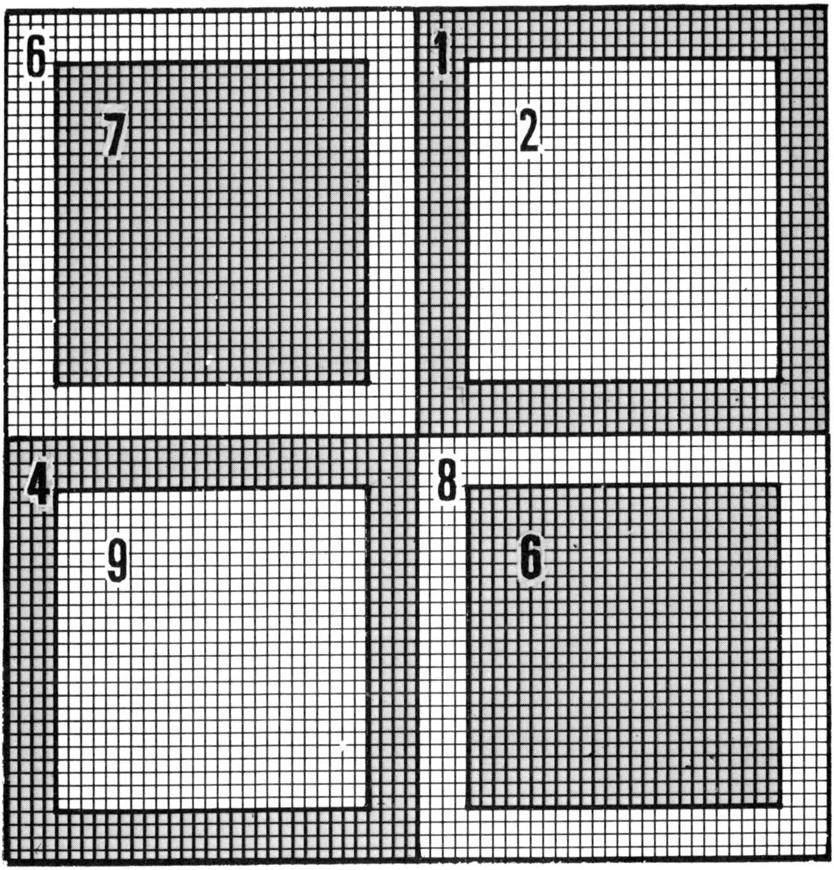

Above: *Squares and circles cushions* (see page 55); left: *Florentine bolster cushion* (see page 50)

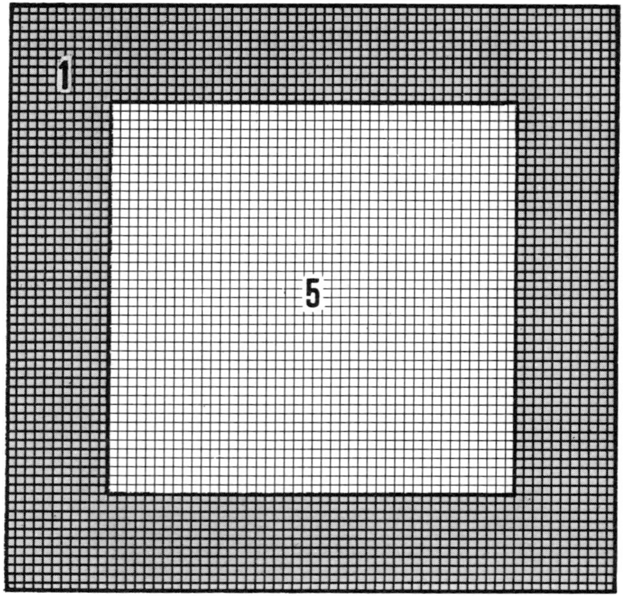

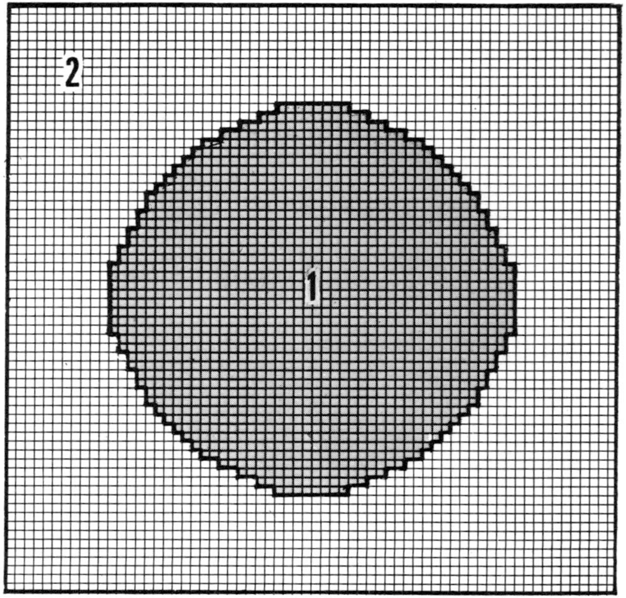

Above and facing page: *Squares and circles* (see page 55)

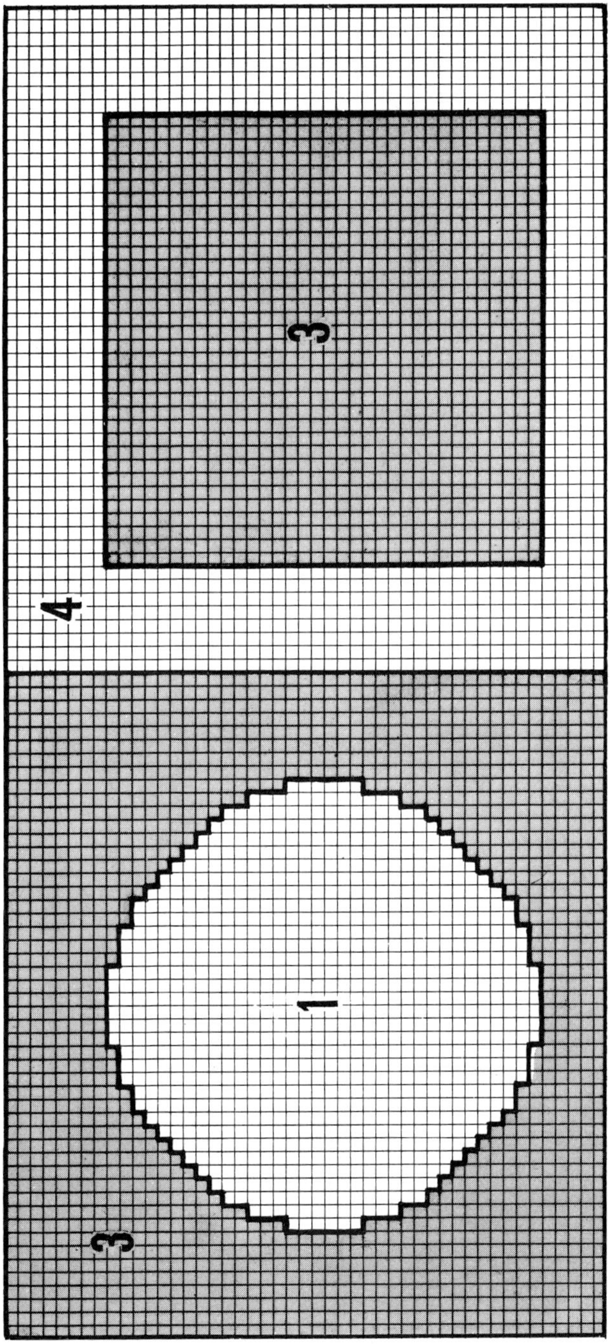
3
4
1
3

INDEX

Abstract cushions, 51–3
Addresses, *115*
Animal silhouettes, 83–5
Apple embroidered cushion, 30–2; table cloth and matching lampshades, 78–80
Appliqué, methods, etc., *71–3*

Back stitch, *118*
Bedspread and rug, 142–5
Bias binding hem, *113*
Blackwork luncheon set, 38–41
Blocking out, *151*
Buttonhole stitch, *117*

Cable stitch, *106*
Canvas work, methods, etc., *42–47*; *bed cover, 47–49*
Chain stitch, *117*, (in crochet) *147*
Chart enlargements, *153–159*
Coil filling stitch, *120*
Colour, *17–18*
Crochet, methods, etc., *122–146*; stitches, *146–152*
Cross stitch, *118*; Double, *119*; *napkins, 19–21, 153–5*; *rug, 98–9*

Diamond stitch, *108*, Crossed, *108*
Double faggot stitch, *119*; feather stitch, *110*
Drawn fabric table set, 27–30

Edge stitch, *90*
Embroidery stitches, *116–121*
Enlarging and reducing designs, *16–17*
Eyelet stitch, *118*

Fabrics, *14*, *43*, *60*, *71*, *86*, *100*; preparation, *15*, *44*, *90*, *102*
Fern stitch, *118*
Flowery smocked nightdress, 102–6
Florentine cushion, 49–51, 156
Four-sided stitch, *120*
Frames, embroidery, *13–14*, *43*, *71*
French knots, *117*
Fringes, *92*
Fringed poncho, 139, 142–3
Fruit and berries table runner, 23–5

Ghiordes knot stitch, *95*
Giant flower cushion, 79, 81–2

Hem stitch, *120*
Honeycomb stitch, *109*

Interlocking Gobelin stitch, *93*

Lace curtain, 123–5
Linked four-sided stitch, *120*
Lion window blind, 75, 77
Long and short stitch, *116*
Lupin and marigold picture, 25–6

Mitred corner, *112*
Mother and daughter dresses, 136–41
Mounting fabrics, *15*, *114*

Needles, *12*, *42*, *59*, *71*, *86*

Outline stitch, *106*

Patchwork, methods, etc., *59–62*; *cushions, 63–9*; *Sweet dreams quilt, 69–70*
Peony bedspread, 37–8
Petal bedspread, 125–134
Pink-flowered bedspread, 34–7
Plait stitch, *90*

Rocking chair cushions, 53–6
Rugs, crochet, *134–6*, *142–5*; needle-made, *86–99*; planning your own design, *87*

Satin stitch, *116*
Scissors, *12*, *13*, *42*, *71*, *86*
Sheaf stitch, *118*
Smocking methods, etc., *100*, *102*; stitches, *106–111*
Soumak stitch, *92*
Spring flower table mats, 31–3
Squares and circles, 55, 57–8, 157–9
Star stitch, *118*
Stem stitch, *117*
Still life in a blue bowl, 73–6
Straight stitch, *116*
Surrey stitch, *94*

Target rag rug, 134–6
Tent stitch, *121*
Transferring designs, *16*
Trellis stitch, *106*
Turkey stitch, *95*

Vandyke stitch, *109*

Water lily table cloth, 22–24
Wave stitch, *107*
Wavy-bordered curtains, 22, 24
Wheat-ear stitch, *121*

Yarns, *14–15*, *43*, *100*; starting and finishing off, *18*, *45*